Oregon Coast Best Places®

A Destination Guide

FROM THE *BEST PLACES* EDITORS

SASQUATCH BOOKS
SEATTLE

Printed in the United States of America.

Distributed in Canada by Raincoast Books Ltd.

Cover design: Karen Schober
Cover map: Rolf Goetzinger
Foldout maps: Word Graphics
Interior design and composition: John D. Berry

Library of Congress Cataloging in Publication Data

Oregon coast best places : a destination guide /
from the Best places editors.

    p. cm. – (Best places destination guides)
Includes index.
ISBN 1-57061-030-4 : $11.95
1. Pacific Coast (Or.) – Guidebooks. I. Series.
F874.3.074 1995
917.904´33 – dc20   95-3788

Sasquatch Books publishes high-quality non-
fiction and children's titles related to the Northwest. For a complete list of our titles, contact us
at the following address.

Sasquatch Books
1008 Western Avenue
Seattle, Washington 98104
(206) 467-4300

Contents

iv   *Acknowledgments*

v   *Preface*

vii   *How to Use This Book*

3   Astoria

17   Gearhart

19   Seaside

26   Cannon Beach

34   Manzanita

41   Garibaldi & Bay City

42   Tillamook & Oceanside

47   Cloverdale & Pacific City

51   Neskowin & Otis

54   Lincoln City

60   Gleneden Beach

63   Depoe Bay

66   Newport

75   Seal Rock

77   Waldport

79   Yachats

89   Florence

97   Reedsport

99   Winchester Bay

102   North Bend

104   Coos Bay

108   Charleston

113   Bandon

125   Port Orford

131   Gold Beach

139   Brookings

147   *Index*

Acknowledgments

Although the *Destination Guides* couldn't have been produced without the countless contributors to our *Best Places* and *Cheap Sleeps* series, there are three people in particular who scouted out the best the Oregon Coast has to offer – beyond where to sleep and where to eat.

Richard Fencsak is a time-tested contributor to the *Best Places* guidebooks. When he's not out checking out the Oregon Coast's best restaurants and lodgings, he's either managing his bike shop in Astoria or mountain biking the backroads of the Coast Range.

Mark Morris remembers his first trip along the Oregon Coast, when finding a good cup of coffee was something akin to seeking the Holy Grail. Morris, an editor of many travel books, currently lives in Portland.

Elizabeth Rhudy, who spent several years editing travel guides, now works for the other side of the business in Portland – a large public-relations firm. This Oregon Coast project proved she hasn't lost touch with her true voice.

Preface

The Sasquatch Books *Best Places* series is unique in that the guidebooks are written by and for locals – which makes them coveted by visitors. The books are designed for travelers who enjoy exploring the bounty of the region, who like out-of-the-way places of high character and individualism, and who take the time to seek out such places. *Best Places* inspectors travel anonymously; we accept no free meals, accommodations, or other complimentary services. Our forthright reviews rate establishments on a scale of zero to four stars and describe the true strengths, foibles, and unique characteristics of each.

Our new *Best Places Destination Guides* are written for those who have always trusted the restaurant and lodging reviews in *Northwest Best Places* but longed for additional suggestions on what to do between dining and reclining. For each destination we've provided *Best Places* selections for restaurants and lodgings. To give you more lodging options for your money, we've added recommended bargain lodgings from our *Northwest Cheap Sleeps*. Then we had our inspectors research each destination thoroughly, consulting myriad regional spies and sources, and collecting local knowledge about the best the area has to offer – from galleries to beaches, concerts to parks. The *Destination Guides* are designed to be chatty and easy to browse, with icons to help you locate your favorite activities.

We like to think the *Destination Guides* are the next best thing to having a friend on the Oregon Coast.

– The Editors

How to Use This Book

ACTIVITIES

 Arts and crafts, *galleries*

 Beaches *(salt water and fresh), swimming, beachcombing*

 Bicycling

 Birdwatching *and other wildlife viewing*

 Boating: *marinas, moorings, boat rentals*

 Camping

 Drinks *(espresso, wine, beer)*

 Dune buggies

 Entertainment: *movies, theater, concerts, performing arts*

 Events: *festivals, fairs, annual festivities*

 Local produce, *farmers' markets, farm products, organic foods*

 Ferries

 Fishing *(salt water and fresh)*

Food shops, *grocery stores, some cafes and pubs*

Golf

 Hikes and walks

 Historic landmarks, *museums, petroglyphs*

 Horseback riding

 Information sources *(newspapers, magazines)*

 Kayaking and canoeing

 Kid-friendly

 Lighthouses

 Music, *concerts, music events*

 Nature, *wilderness areas, nature walks*

 Parks

 Picnic areas

 River rafting *and river cruises*

 Scuba diving

 Seals & sea lions

 Seminars, *workshops, ecotours, educational activities*

Shellfish *(clams, oysters, mussels)*: *foraging and buying*

 Shops: *clothing, books, antiques, souvenirs*

 Tennis

 Transportation: *car rental, planes, buses*

 Views, *scenic driving tours, attractions*

 Whalewatching

 Windsurfing, *boardsurfing*

RECOMMENDED RESTAURANTS AND LODGINGS

At the end of each town section you'll find restaurants and lodgings recommended by our *Best Places* editors.

 Restaurants

Lodgings

Rating System: Establishments with stars have been rated on a scale of zero to four. Ratings are based on uniqueness, enjoyability, value, loyalty of local clientele, excellence of cooking, performance measured against goals, and professionalism of service.

In addition, we've recommended bargain lodgings – the best place for the best price. These are usually $60 or under for one night's lodging for two.

✦	A bargain lodging
(no stars)	Worth knowing about, if nearby
☆	A good place
☆☆	Some wonderful qualities
☆☆☆	Distinguished, many outstanding features
☆☆☆☆	The very best in the region
Unrated	New or undergoing major changes

Price Range: When prices range between two categories (for example, moderate to expensive), the lower one is given. Call ahead to verify. All of our bargain lodgings are $60 or under for two.

$$$ **Expensive.** Indicates a tab of more than $75 for dinner for two, including wine (but not tip), and more than $90 for one night's lodging for two.

$$ **Moderate.** Falls between expensive and inexpensive.

$ **Inexpensive.** Indicates a tab of less than $25 for dinner, and less than $60 for lodgings for two.

The
Oregon
Coast

Oregon Coast

Mist-enshrouded headlands, golden stretches of pristine beach, river estuaries rich in marine life. Coastal fishing villages, local arts and crafts, and a plethora of inns, motels, campgrounds, and resorts. Is it any wonder that the Oregon Coast has become one of the Northwest's prime destinations, for locals and visitors alike? With Highway 101 weaving the length of the coast, offering not only easy access but also countless dramatic views, tourism has become a major industry where fishing and logging once ruled.

The most development has occurred along the northern, Portland-accessible section of coast, an area marked by dramatic capes, rivers spilling out of forested coastal mountains, and long expanses of misty beach. Fishing villages alternate with tourist towns, and many of the residents – an eclectic mix of artists, retirees, upwardly mobile surfers, fishermen, loggers, and entrepreneurs trying to escape city life – are seeking a consensus on the appropriate amount of development. During summer, crowds throng the streets of Cannon Beach or line up

Showing considerable foresight, the state of Oregon decreed public access to all of its beaches sacrosanct; in addition, many stretches of the coastline are preserved as state parks.

to visit the Sea Lion Caves, while RVs compete with bicyclists and logging trucks for space on the twisting curves of 101. But the attractions are hard to resist, so the crowds keep coming. With a little effort, however, you can still escape the masses. And in the "off-season" – when the ocean is at its dramatic best – the crowds disappear.

The southern part of the Oregon Coast maintains a slower pace year-round. In fact, a long succession of state parks and 50 miles of the Oregon Dunes National Recreation Area ensure that this paradise will not be subjected to the overdevelopment that has ravaged sections of the northern coast. With the exception of the stretch between Yachats and Coos Bay, the south coast remains a wild place with a singular sense of openness.

Astoria

"We ain't quaint!" is a popular bumper sticker in this town of 10,000 residents, who collectively claim the title of first American settlement west of the Rockies. And while Astoria features a world-class maritime museum and numerous other historical attractions, including a hillside dotted with

Founded in 1811 by John Jacob Astor's fur-trading company, Astoria really dates to the mid-19th century, when it began to thrive as a cannery town and shipping center. By the turn of the century, Astoria boasted a rip-roaring, Sodom and Gomorrah-type waterfront with brothels and bars galore, and a reputation as shanghai central for unwary sailors. Salmon was king, and as many as 36 canneries operated on the lower Columbia. Now, there are none.

restored 19th-century-era Victorian homes, it continues to sport a blue-collar image.

Astoria's reverence for the past blends nicely with its working-class present. The town is home to an active commercial fishing fleet, and many people are still employed in the wood products industry. Oceangoing freighters and tankers ply the Columbia River — right past a bustling downtown waterfront — on their way between Portland and the Pacific. Espresso bars have become de rigueur, but unlike many other coastal communities, T-shirt shops have yet to replace core businesses here. Astoria hasn't stood still waiting for the tourists to arrive, but they're visiting in ever greater numbers, precisely because the town isn't just another glitzy tourist destination.

▶ **City Walk.** The best way to "do" Astoria is on foot. Begin at the base of 17th Street, adjacent to the maritime museum, and head west along the river. The 14th Street Pier allows views of working tugboats and the goings-on of the Columbia River Bar and River Pilots. (Astoria is the only city on the West Coast where you can observe pilots getting on and off oceangoing vessels.) Eight blocks

Up the hillside from the waterfront is a treasure trove of Victorian residences. Head up 17th Street (it gets steep!); between Franklin and Jerome Avenues are myriad examples of 19th-century homes, restored to their former splendor.

away, at Sixth Street River Park, is a covered observation tower (always open) where you can view river commerce and watch sea lions and seals search for a free lunch.

 Fort Clatsop National Memorial (6 miles southwest of Astoria off Highway 101; (503) 861-2471) recreates Lewis and Clark's 1805–06 winter encampment. Besides the audiovisuals and exhibits at the visitors center, there are living history displays (firings of black-powder muskets, construction of dugout canoes) in the summer.

 Reading Material. Pint-size Parnassus Books (234 10th Street; (503) 325-1363) packs a lot of good reading into a small space. Godfather's Books (1108 Commercial Street; (503) 325-8143) offers indoor seating, coffee drinks, and such.

 The Ricciardi Gallery (108 10th Street; (503) 325-5450) displays the city's finest selection of regional art. This is where the locals hang out to enjoy espresso, juices, desserts, homemade soup, and a great selection of reading material. On sunny days, this is the choice sidewalk-table hangout.

One hundred years ago, Astoria boasted an extraordinarily high number of bars and churches. The churches are still here, but most of the waterfront "dens of iniquity" have long since passed into folklore. What remains is, fortunately, considerably more sedate.

 Astoria Museums. The Columbia River Maritime Museum (1792 Marine Drive; (503) 325-2323) features a Great Hall with restored small craft and a panoramic, balcony view of the Columbia River. Seven thematic galleries depict different aspects of the region's maritime heritage. The lightship *Columbia*, the last of its kind on the Pacific coast, is moored outside (a tour is included in the admission price).

The Flavel House (Eighth and Duane Streets; (503) 325-2563), named after a prominent 19th-century businessman and the founder of the first successful Columbia River Bar Pilots organization, is Astoria's finest example of ornate Queen Anne architecture. The Heritage Museum (1618 Exchange Street; (503) 325-2203) is a beautifully restored building that once housed the city hall and jail. Both museums are operated by the Clatsop County Historical Society and feature local historical displays.

 Great soups, salads, and sandwiches can be had at Peri's (915 Commercial Street; (503) 325-5560), frequented by the downtown lunch crowd and the local press. In addition to sandwiches, killer desserts are available at Peter Pan Market

(712 Niagara; (503) 325-2143). Nearby Niagara Park offers an outdoor eating venue.

 Josephson's Smokehouse (106 Marine Drive, (503) 325-2190) prepares superb alder-smoked salmon, tuna, and sturgeon.

 Farm Fresh. Astoria's best sources for fresh fruits and veggies are Columbia Fruit & Produce (598 Bond; (503) 325-4045), a kind of an indoor farmers' market that occasionally offers local organic produce, and the Community Store (1389 Duane; (503) 325-0027), which features a selection of healthy packaged munchies.

 Theater productions, including the summer's *Shanghaied in Astoria,* are staged year-round at the Astor Street Opry Company (1405 Commercial Street; (503) 325-6104).

 The Scandinavian Midsummer Fest – an annual celebration of the city's heritage – includes ethnic foods, dancing, and music. It's held in June at Astoria High School; (503) 325-0003.

Reputedly the oldest continuously operating water-related festival in the Northwest, the Astoria Regatta features boat races, parades, music, and lots of additional hoopla. Held in mid-August; (503) 325-5123; locations vary.

 Sports-oriented Merry Time (995 Marine Drive; (503) 325-5606) has a healthy selection of microbrews and the most TV sets in town. You can even bet on the ponies here. Cafe Uniontown (218 W Marine Drive; (503) 325-8707) offers a comfortable setting and acoustic music (on most weekends).

 Astorians like to call the woods that wrap around the south and east sides of their town an "urban forest." You can access it at either end of the Cathedral Tree Trail, so named because it leads to a 300-year-old spruce, a remnant of coastal forests of the past. Pick up the well-marked trailhead at the Astoria Column parking lot, or off Irving Avenue at 29th Street.

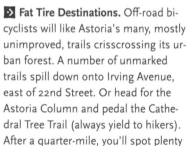 **Fat Tire Destinations.** Off-road bicyclists will like Astoria's many, mostly unimproved, trails crisscrossing its urban forest. A number of unmarked trails spill down onto Irving Avenue, east of 22nd Street. Or head for the Astoria Column and pedal the Cathedral Tree Trail (always yield to hikers). After a quarter-mile, you'll spot plenty

Favorite espresso
stop: "Who **doesn't**
go to the Ricciardi
Gallery?"
– Sue Borgardt,
businesswoman,
Astoria city
commissioner

of offshoot opportunities. Warrenton's
Fort Stevens State Park provides both
paved and unpaved trails and uncrowded roads. Stop in at Bikes & Beyond (1089 Marine Drive; (503) 325-
2961) for information and free Oregon
Coast bike maps. Ask the owners
about their favorite on- and off-road
biking routes. In summer, rent bikes
at Hammond's Fort Stevens Bike
Rental (at the four-way stop, no
phone).

▶ Paddling Destinations. Canoeists
and kayakers can put in at the Astoria
Yacht Club (on Young's Bay, underneath the old Young's Bay Bridge), the
Columbia River's East-end Mooring
Basin (off Leif Erickson Drive, on the
east end of Astoria), and the John Day
boat ramp (off Highway 30, 5 miles
east of Astoria). The latter, which
leads into the John Day River, is a local
" 'yakers" favorite and a gunkholer's
paradise. It traverses under a railroad
trestle and into a calm section of the
Columbia dotted with islands populated by eagles, ospreys, and four-
legged wildlife.

▶ When you're surrounded by water
on three sides, you know there must
be some fish out there. Angling from
a boat is your best bet for Columbia

Although Victoria Dahl's (2921 Marine Drive; (503) 325-7109) may look like just another antique shop, it's much more. Antiques are for sale, but so is some awfully good food, mostly Italian. Sample anything with seafood.

River estuary or ocean fishing. A number of area charter-boat operators offer salmon, sturgeon, and bottom-fishing excursions, as well as specialty river cruises. A search for the right boat might begin at Tiki Charters (at Astoria's West-end Basin; (503) 325-7818). Numerous rivers provide excellent opportunities for catching salmon, trout, and steelhead. Astoria fishing guru Bob Ellsberg recommends the Klatskanine River (east of Astoria, along Highway 202) for seasonal salmon and steelhead angling, and Cullaby Lake (off Highway 101, 11 miles south of Astoria) for bass and trout.

 Eagles and Elk. Approximately 48 eagles feed and roost at the Twilight Eagle Sanctuary, 8 miles east of Astoria (off Highway 30 on Burnside Road). The Jewell Meadows Wildlife Area (26 miles east of town on Highway 202; (503) 755-2264), with its rolling meadows, is at times populated by hundreds of elk, including majestic bulls with enormous racks.

  Surf the Wind or Fish the Surf. Fort Stevens State Park (off Highway 101 and Ridge Road, 10 miles northwest of Astoria; (503) 861-1671) is a 3,500-acre outdoor wonderland of forest trails,

The 166-step climb up the Astoria Column, atop Coxcomb Hill, presents a panoramic view that's particularly lovely at sunset. If the climb's too much for you, the parking area offers a fine view, too.

uncrowded beaches, running and biking paths, and a freshwater lake, suitable for swimming and fishing. With 604 campsites, Fort Stevens is Oregon's largest publicly owned campground. Summer reservations are encouraged.

Within the park you'll find good razor clamming (check with park officials concerning regulations); choice windsurfing (in the ocean off the south jetty, or in nearby Trestle Bay); and productive surf fishing (particularly from the jetty; no license required, except for salmon). There's also a military museum and a shipwreck (the rusting hulk of the *Peter Iredale*, wrecked in 1906).

 The South Jetty lookout tower in Fort Stevens State Park is perched at Oregon's northwesternmost point, providing a supreme storm- and whale-watching spot. It also marks the start of the Oregon Coast Trail, which traverses sandy beaches and forested headlands all the way to the California border.

  It's way out of town, but Camp 18 (U.S. Highway 26 at milepost 18; (503) 755-1818) is a combination loggers' theme park and chowhounds' fantasy.

Favorite Oregon
Coast restaurants:
three cafes – the
Columbian in Astoria,
Midtown in Cannon
Beach, and Blue Sky in
Manzanita.

– Mary Blake, director
of Seaside's Sunset
Empire Park and Rec-
reation District

The decor: long, imposing tables sit beneath a towering, open-beamed ceiling; chain saws, hand tools, and logging photos line the walls. The interest quotient of the logging apparatus outside is, alone, worth a visit. Portions are huge and lean heavily toward meat 'n' potatoes. One piece of advice: Don't sass your waitress.

 The Lewis and Clark Interpretive Center – just across the river at Fort Canby in Ilwaco, Washington – provides the perfect vantage point for viewing the notorious Columbia River bar. In winter, Mother Nature struts her stuff as 15- to 30-foot swells, looking like an invading tidal-wave army, march over the bar into the river.

Restaurants

COLUMBIAN CAFE

The Columbian keeps getting more publicity (and therefore more crowds), but this small, vegetarian-oriented cafe continues to be Astoria's best bet for good grub. Be prepared for long waits, cramped quarters, erratic hours, uneven service, an eccentric chef, and great food – perhaps the finest seafood and pasta dishes on the Oregon Coast. If you're feeling frisky, order the

Astoria Coffee Company (1154 Commercial Street; (503) 325-7173) serves the best joe-to-go in town. Convivial owners Peg Davis and Rick Murray, former Seattleites, are a good source for local info.

Chef's Mercy, an eclectic combination of the day's best (and freshest) ingredients. *Corner of 11th St and Marine Dr; (503) 325-2233; 1114 Marine Dr, Astoria; $; beer and wine; no credit cards; checks OK; breakfast, lunch Mon–Sat, dinner Wed–Sat.*

CAFE UNIONTOWN

The latest incarnation of a restaurant that has gone through several, the Uniontown is the spot for decent food, good service, and pleasant ambience. You probably won't be overwhelmed by anything here (except perhaps the portions), but if you're looking for halibut or salmon (in season, and correctly cooked), you've come to the right place. *Underneath the interstate bridge on Marine Dr; (503) 325-8708; 218 W Marine Dr, Astoria; $$; full bar; AE, DIS, MC, V; checks OK; lunch, dinner Tues–Sat.*

THE SHIP INN

An Astoria waterfront institution, this congenial and crowded eatery, operated by English expatriates Jill and Fenton Stokeld, is home to some great fish 'n' chips — double-dipped in a delicately seasoned batter and never overcooked. Somehow, neither fish nor chips are greasy, and both go

Question most frequently asked by tourists: "Where's the beach?"

down easily with a pint of Watney's (on tap). Ask for a window table, where you can watch bar and river pilots get on and off oceangoing vessels in the river channel just a hundred yards away. A hospitable bar affords a cozy waiting area; no reservations accepted. *On the west end of town, on the waterfront at the foot of 2nd St; (503) 325-0033; 1 2nd St, Astoria; $$; full bar; MC, DIS, V; checks OK; lunch, dinner every day.*

RIO CAFE   Unrated

Good Mexican restaurants on the coast are as rare as snowfall in Tijuana. The new cheerful Rio, which offers an eclectic mix from central Mexico, is an exception. Everything is prepared from scratch, and the salsa and chips (huge, crispy, white-corn flour affairs called *totopos*) are always fresh. Most of the options on the selective menu – from Tres Cosas (corn tortillas, beans, and rice) to a scintillatingly hot Pescade Rojo (sole or cod lightly breaded and grilled with a red-chili and garlic sauce) – are impressive. *159 9th Street, Astoria, OR 97103; (503) 325-2409; $; beer and wine; MC, V; lunch Mon–Sat, dinner Thurs–Sat.*

Lodgings

ASTORIA INN BED AND BREAKFAST

No doubt about it, this 1890s Victorian farmhouse is the best *situated* B&B in town, located above the city with a sweeping view of the Columbia. The grounds are meticulously landscaped, just steps away from trails leading up into the woods – very green and alive, very Astoria. There are three handsomely furnished rooms, an out-of-the-wind verandah, and a cozy library. *Irving Ave and 34th St; (503) 325-8153; 3391 Irving Ave, Astoria, OR 97103; $$; MC, V; checks OK.*

CREST MOTEL

With 40 rooms situated on a forested bluff overlooking the Columbia River, the Crest offers the best motel view in town. It's at the east edge of Astoria and therefore quiet – except for the sound of foghorns, which on winter evenings can be heard bellowing up the hillside from the ship traffic below. Recline in lawn chairs in the large backyard and enjoy a bird's-eye view of the in- and outgoing tankers and freighters, or unwind in a gazebo-enclosed whirlpool. Pets are welcome, and one section is designated nonsmoking. *2 miles east of downtown; (503) 325-3141; 5366 Leif Erikson Dr, Astoria, OR 97103; $$; AE, DC, DIS, MC, V; checks OK.*

CLEMENTINE'S BED AND BREAKFAST ¢

Here's a reasonably priced addition to Astoria's burgeoning bed-and-breakfast scene. Clementine's is an Italianate Victorian located on the edge of downtown, partway up hyper-steep Eighth Street. Your hosts, Judith and Cliff Taylor (she's a master gardener and cooking instructor; he's into boats), are enthusiastic about north coast happenings. All rooms have private baths and fresh garden flowers. A separate vacation rental that sleeps six fetches $85 (but no breakfast). *8th and Exchange; (503) 325-2005; 847 Exchange St, Astoria, OR 97103; $; AE, DIS, MC, V; checks OK.*

FRANKLIN STREET STATION ☆

The location, 2 blocks from downtown on a rather ordinary street, could be better, but the house itself has style and elegance. A shipbuilder constructed the home at the turn of the century; lavish woodwork attests to his fondness for local forest products. The interior is quite frilly with

Victoriana. Three rooms open onto distant river views, and two have outside decks. An attic room, the Captain's Quarters, has the best view and its own living room. *Between 11th and 12th on Franklin; (503) 325-4314 or (800) 448-1098; 1140 Franklin Ave, Astoria, OR 97103; $$; MC, V; checks OK.*

ROSEBRIAR HOTEL   ¢

The Rosebriar has done time as a private residence, a convent, and a halfway house for the mentally disabled. Now in its finest reincarnation, the place is a rambling 11-room inn. All guest rooms are generally small, but beautifully furnished and meticulously clean. The common rooms are spacious and homey, and the outside grounds afford a gardenlike setting. *Franklin and 14th; (503) 325-7427 or (800) 487-0224; 636 14th St, Astoria, OR 97103; $; MC, V; checks OK.*

Gearhart

Mostly residential, Gearhart exemplifies Oregon Coast architecture, with an assortment of beachfront, weathered-wood homes in shades of white and gray. Some of the dwellings are substantial, built by fashionable

Gearhart has a Martha's Vineyard look, with a wide, white-sand beach backed by lovely dunes partially covered with bunchgrass. Razor clamming is popular.

One of the coziest indoor locales around is the lounge of Gearhart's Oceanside Restaurant (1200 N Marion; (503) 738-7789). The oceanfront setting overlooks a less crowded stretch of dunes and beach. The view is spectacular, especially at night, with white-capped waves breaking against a moonlit sky.

Portlanders when the coast was being discovered. Gearhart now showcases an interesting blend of well-to-do weekenders and local fishermen, artists, and retirees.

 Gearhart Golf Course, opened in 1892, is the second-oldest course in the West — a 6,089-yard layout with sandy soil that dries quickly; open to the public, (503) 738-3538.

 The dunes at the end of Pacific Way are the perfect place to watch a sunset. There's even a bench and a gently sloping trail to the beach.

 Don't miss A Great Shop (576 Pacific Way; (503) 738-3540), which features unusual but functional knickknacks, from gourmet food items to children's toys and books.

Restaurants

PACIFIC WAY BAKERY AND CAFE

This airy cafe, with hardwood floors, lots of windows, hip service, cool sounds, and plenty of espresso, is the only restaurant in downtown (such as it is) Gearhart. It continues to thrive on a mix of suspender-and-clam-shovel locals and out-of-town "gearheads," the BMW-and-summer-beachfront-home crowd. They come to hang out, hobnob, and sample the best pastries and breads the north coast has to offer. *Downtown Gearhart, corner of Cottage and Pacific Way; (503) 738-0245; 601 Pacific Way, Gearhart; $; beer and wine; MC, V; checks OK; breakfast, lunch Wed–Sun.*

Seaside

One hundred years ago, affluent beachgoers rode Columbia River steamers to Astoria from Portland, then hopped a stagecoach to Seaside, the Oregon Coast's first resort town. It seems the place has become more crowded every year since. On any summer weekend, the traffic lines up for a long way on Highway 101 and at the intersection of Broadway and Holladay, the town's main thorough-fares. The crowds mill along Broadway, eyeing the entertainment parlors, the sweet-treat concessions, and the bumper cars, then emerge at the Prom, the 2-mile-long cement "boardwalk" that's ideal for strolling (but watch out for skateboarders, roller-bladers, and bicyclists).

▶ The rugged 7-mile hike over Tillamook Head, part of Ecola State Park, is one of the coast's most rewarding for spectacular vistas,

Lately, Seaside has been undergoing a restaurant renaissance. Two restaurants on Broadway — Miguel's (412 Broadway; (503) 738-0171), a pint-size Tex-Mex eatery with great seafood-stuffed tacos, and Little New Yorker (604 Broadway; (503) 738-5992), an East Coast–inspired Italian diner with two-fisted meatball sandwiches — are part of the picture.

including a view of the Tillamook Rock Lighthouse. The trailhead begins at the end of Sunset Boulevard at the town's south end and finishes at Indian Beach and (farther still) Ecola Point, near Cannon Beach.

Another strenuous but sensational hike begins 14 miles east at Saddle Mountain State Park, off Highway 26. A narrow, winding road leads to the trailhead, which proceeds 2½ miles — at times steep and gravelly — to the 3,283-foot summit. On a clear day, the ocean, the Columbia River, the Coast Range, and even Mount St. Helens are visible. Klootchy Creek Park (along Highway 26, 2 miles east of the Cannon Beach junction) claims the world's largest Sitka spruce, and another opportunity to access the Necanicum River. There's a favored fishing hole right under the bridge.

▶ The Sand Dollar Gallery (Sand Dollar Square on Broadway; (503) 738-3491) features Northwest arts and crafts.

▶ Charlie's Turnaround Books (111 Broadway; (503) 738-3211), a block from the beach, affords an opportunity to browse the shelves and sip espresso.

Cafe Espresso (600 Broadway; (503) 738-6169) is the best spot in Seaside for joe-to-go.

>> Local author and outdoorsman Bob Ellsberg calls the Necanicum the north coast's best year-round fishing stream. Salmon, steelhead, and trout are all routinely pulled out of this swift-moving waterway, and access is very good. You can fish off of, or just below, the Avenue U bridge (adjacent to Highway 101 on the south side of town). Follow Avenue U 4 blocks west to the ocean for razor clamming or surf fishing.

>> The Point (along Sunset Boulevard) offers the finest left-handed surfing waves in Oregon. A rock-strewn beach, radical riptides, and an overprotective contingent of locals limit water time for all but the experienced. Just a half-mile north, the Cove offers a more forgiving wave, although the rocks are still plentiful. Cleanline Surf Company (719 First Avenue; (503) 738-7888) is a good source for ocean-play equipment and info.

>> Oceangoing kayakers also frequent the Cove (along Sunset Boulevard), whose waters are approachable via an adjacent sandy beach.

>> Quatat Marine Park, which parallels the Necanicum River, is the setting for many free events. There are concerts every Saturday afternoon in

Emmanuel's (104 Broadway; (503) 738-7038) purveys tasty seafood and pasta specials, but you can't be in a hurry here, since service can sometimes be slow.

summer – everything from folk to jazz to grunge – all part of the "Where the Stars Play" music series sponsored by the Sunset Empire Park and Recreation District; (503) 738-3311.

> The Turnaround, on the Prom (at the western end of Broadway), is a great place to watch the sunset – and other people watching the sunset.

Restaurants

DOOGER'S

Where do you eat in a town full of taffy concessions, hot dog stands, and bumper cars? Frankly, there aren't many choices, but your best bet is Dooger's – as the line outside on weekends (and sometimes during the week) will attest. Inside, it's a clean, smokeless, unkitschy family place with friendly service. Stick with the simpler offerings, like chowder and the local catch. There's another, larger Dooger's in Cannon Beach (1371 S Hemlock, (503) 436-2225). *Broadway and Franklin; (503) 738-3773; 505 Broadway, Seaside; $$; beer and wine; MC, V; local checks only; lunch, dinner every day.*

VISTA SEA CAFE

Inside Vista Sea Cafe you'll find a pleasant respite from the oft-frenzied

Sure it's glitzy, but the Shilo Inn's bar offers comfortable seating and an ocean-front view along with the glitz. There's live music every weekend and a diverse crowd to rub shoulders with (30 N Prom; (503) 738-9571 or (800) 222-2244).

crowd. Squeeze into a wooden booth and sample one of their pizzas. Choose from tons of toppings, including some unorthodox cheeses (Montrachet, Oregon blue), to create your mouthwatering pie on a hefty, chewy crust – slightly light on the sauce (request more). *On the corner of Broadway and Columbia; (503) 738-8108; 150 Broadway, Seaside; $; beer and wine; MC, V; local checks only; lunch, dinner every day.*

Lodgings

THE BOARDING HOUSE

Fir tongue-and-groove walls, beamed ceilings, and wood paneling recall traditional boardinghouse decor at this turn-of-the-century Victorian. The house fronts Seaside's busy Holladay Drive, and the backyard slopes gently to the Necanicum River – convenient and close to the beach. All six guest rooms have a wicker-and-wood beachy feeling. There's also a miniature Victorian cottage that sleeps up to six people. Full breakfasts included. *N Holladay and 3rd at 208 N Holladay Dr; (503) 738-9055; PO Box 573, Seaside, OR 97138; $$; MC, V; checks OK.*

BEACHWOOD BED AND BREAKFAST

This 1900 Craftsman-style lodging, just a block east of the beach, is nicely ensconced in a quiet residential neighborhood, nestled in among coastal pines, an easy walk from downtown. The Astor Room is outfitted with an unusual sleigh-shaped bed and a comfy window seat with a peek of the Pacific. The first-floor Holladay Suite has a frilly canopy bed, a gas fireplace, and Jacuzzi. No children or pets. *Beach Dr and Ave G; (503) 738-9585; 671 Beach Dr, Seaside, OR 97138; $$; MC, V; checks OK; (closed mid-Nov to mid-Feb).*

SHILO INN (SEASIDE OCEANFRONT)

We tend to be wary of glitzy establishments that hog the shoreline, but this one has a good reputation. The setting, of course, is superb; the lobby is stylish and mirrored; the prices are stratospheric. But all the amenities expected in a resort hotel are here, from an indoor pool to a workout room. The choicest rooms (graced with fireplaces, kitchens, and private patios) face the ocean. The Shilo frequently hosts conventions, so it's not the place to get away from the hubbub of urban life. *N Prom and Broadway at Seaside's Turnaround; (503) 738-9571 or (800) 222-2244; 30 N Prom, Seaside, OR 97138; $$$; AE, DC, DIS, MC, V; checks OK.*

RIVERSIDE INN BED AND BREAKFAST ¢

The Riverside continues to be Seaside's best bargain for traditional-style lodging. It's comfortable, spacious, and clean, with adjacent cottages. While the front faces bustling Holladay Drive, the rear recedes gracefully to the Necanicum River. A large riverfront deck provides opportunities for fishing, semi-secluded sunbathing, or relaxing. The beach is just 3½ blocks away. *On Holladay Drive; (503) 738-8254 or (800) 862-6151; 430 S Holladay Drive, Seaside, OR 97138; $; DIS, MC, V; checks OK.*

SEASIDE INN AND INTERNATIONAL HOSTEL ¢

It was only a matter of time until resort-minded Seaside welcomed a European-style hostel. This reconverted motel features traditional dormitory-style sleeping quarters (45 beds), some private rooms, shared bathroom facilities, and a large, well-equipped communal kitchen. There's an in-house espresso bar and outside decks, and the Necanicum River flows past the backyard. Unlike traditional hostels, you don't have to leave during the day. *N Holladay and 9th; (503) 738-7911; 930 N Holladay Drive, Seaside, OR 97138; $; MC, V; no checks.*

Cannon Beach (including Tolovana Park)

In warm weather, locals and tourists alike may be found relaxing on the porch outside Osburn's Ice Creamery & Deli (240 N Hemlock; (503) 436-2234).

Cannon Beach is an artsy community with a hip, upscale ambience and a love/hate relationship with the ever-increasing tourist hordes that converge on the town year-round, mainly because there's a lot to like. Strict building codes ensure that only aesthetically pleasing structures are built (usually of cedar and weathered wood). Galleries, crafts shops, and espresso parlors line either side of Hemlock Street, where meandering visitors rub shoulders with the coastal intelligentsia. The main draw continues to be the wide, inviting beach, which, fortunately, remains unchanged and among the prettiest anywhere.

▶ Galleries abound in the Cannon Beach area, all on Hemlock Street, the main drag. Three especially good ones are the White Bird (251 N Hemlock; (503) 436-2681), which features a variety of arts and crafts; the Haystack Gallery (183 N Hemlock; (503) 436-2547), with a wide range of prints and photography; and Jeffrey Hull Watercolors (in Sandpiper Square, 178 N Hemlock; (503) 436-2600), a collection of delicately brushed seascapes. The Cannon Beach Arts Association Gallery (1064 N Hemlock; (503) 436-0744) features local artists.

 Sweet treats, right out of one of the few remaining brick, oil-fired hearth ovens on the West Coast, are available at the Cannon Beach Bakery (144 N Hemlock; (503) 436-2592). Hane's Bakerie (1064 N Hemlock; (503) 436-0120) offers intricate fruit and cheese croissants and the town's best breads.

 A good browse can be had at the Cannon Beach Book Company (132 N Hemlock; (503) 436-1301).

 Locals rely on the *Upper Left Edge* (free at many businesses) newspaper for town news and a cultural calendar, as well as a tide table.

 At Wayfarer (on the beach at Ocean and Gower, adjacent to the Surfsand Resort; (503) 436-1108), the food's nothing to brag about, but the beachfront setting and the views of Haystack Rock and the Pacific can't be beat. In downtown, head for Bill's Tavern (188 N Hemlock; (503) 436-2202), the hot spot for music and gab.

 Haystack Rock, one of the world's largest coastal monoliths, dominates the long, sandy stretch. At low tide you can observe rich marine life in the tidal pools, or take a 5-mile beach walk to Arch Cape (always consult a tide table beforehand). If you didn't attempt the trail over Tillamook Head from Seaside, try it from the north end of Cannon Beach. You can pick it up at a number of places within Ecola State Park – which also offers fabulous views and quiet picnic areas.

 Three-wheelers are popular on the beach, mountain bikes on logging roads and trails. You can rent either at Mike's Bike Shop (248 N Spruce; (503) 436-1266).

 Tiny Elk Creek, which merges with the Pacific just west of downtown, offers good trout and steelhead fishing. Some of the best trout holes can be found by hiking upcreek, on the east side of Highway 101.

 Surfers favor the "Needles" beachbreak, just south of Haystack

Sculpture aficionado and longtime local Jeff Hull's top-choice art finds are Cannon Beach's Bronze Coast Gallery (231 N Hemlock; (503) 436-1055) and Valley Bronze of Oregon (in Sandpiper Square; (503) 436-2118) – where "you'll find cast bronze sculptures with an Old West motif."

Rock, and the right-handed waves at Indian Beach, within Ecola State Park.

> June's Sandcastle Day, a contest drawing sand sculptors from throughout the Northwest and Canada, has become Cannon Beach's busiest day. The crowds, and the traffic, are horrendous. If you visit during Sandcastle Day, get here early, and don't even consider driving or parking downtown. Leave your vehicle at the Tolovana Wayside (off S Hemlock, in Tolovana Park) and walk the beach into town. Be sure to reserve lodging well in advance. For information, contact the Cannon Beach Chamber of Commerce, (503) 436-2623.

Restaurants

CAFE DE LA MER

★★★

Husband-and-wife owners Ron Schiffman and Pat Noonan have transformed a post-'60s coffeehouse into an upscale cafe that has won a considerable following. It's a little pretentious, but that's beginning to mellow (thanks to some well chosen staff). The food continues to shine: seafood, simply and perfectly prepared, is the cafe's raison d'être. Entrées can be as unorthodox as

"At the end of the
summer, the tourists
are in such a hurry
to have a good time,
they forget that
they're here to
relax."

– Mimi Kauffman,
owner, Midtown Cafe

scallops and shrimp sautéed with
filberts or as traditional as a lusty
bouillabaisse. Desserts can be out
of this world, and so can the prices.
*Hemlock and Dawes; (503) 436-1179;
1287 S Hemlock St, Cannon Beach;
$$$; beer and wine; AE, MC, V; local
checks only; dinner Wed-Sat (days vary
in winter).*

THE BISTRO

Once inside, you'll appreciate the
intimate, removed setting at this, per-
haps the least pretentious fine dining
establishment on the north coast.
Matt and Anita Dueber know where
to procure the finest local ingredients
(from their greenhouse next door,
for instance), and every four-course
dinner is substantial, tasty, and rea-
sonably priced. You may start with
an antipasto plate, then move on to
a delicate soup, then a simple salad.
From the entrées you'll choose from
the usual shellfish dishes, or fresh
halibut, or a tomatoey fish stew with
every kind of seafood on the menu
thrown in. We've heard reports of un-
professional service, but have encoun-
tered only the opposite. *Opposite
Spruce in downtown Cannon Beach;
(503) 436-2661; 263 N Hemlock, Can-
non Beach; $$; full bar; MC, V; local*

The Midtown Cafe's most extraordinary pie is known around Cannon Beach as "Haystack High Apple Pie," because it's filled with a huge amount of apples. How does chef Mimi Kauffman get the pie to bake up so high? "I sit on the apples."

checks only; dinner every day (days vary in winter).

MIDTOWN CAFE

Cannon Beachers don't like the fact that the secret's out about their favorite hangout. There are just not enough stools for everyone. Grab a fresh bagel when they're available, then hunker down for some frittatas, nitrate-free bacon, or the tofeta – a scramble of tofu, feta cheese, onions, and spices. Midday at the Midtown features almost legendary burritos, as well as scrumptious soups and sands. Don't miss the lip-smackin'-good fruit smoothies, and be on the lookout for the incredibly luscious Jamaican stew. *6 blocks south of downtown; (503) 436-1016; 1235 S Hemlock, Cannon Beach; $; beer and wine; no credit cards; checks OK; breakfast, lunch Wed-Sun (closed Jan).*

LAZY SUSAN CAFE

Very Oregon. Definitely Cannon Beach. Everyone in town seems to gather at this airy, sunny, double-deck restaurant in a courtyard opposite the Coaster Theater. The interior is bright with natural wood, plants hanging from the balcony, and local art on the walls. Breakfast is the best time here,

The Coaster Theater
in Cannon Beach (108
N Hemlock; (503) 436-
1242) hosts year-
round live entertain-
ment, including tour-
ing musicians and
theater productions.

when you can order omelets, oatmeal, waffles topped with fresh fruit and yogurt, and excellent coffee to prolong your stay. Expect long waits on sunny weekends. *Coaster Square; (503) 436-2816; 126 N Hemlock, Cannon Beach; $; beer and wine; no credit cards; local checks only; breakfast, lunch Wed-Mon (days vary in winter).*

Lodgings

STEPHANIE INN

☆☆

It's new, it's gorgeous, and its elegance of a New England country inn distinguishes the Stephanie Inn on the Oregon Coast. The oceanfront location is not isolated, but there's a definite sense of privacy here. Inside, the emphasis is on pampered and purposeful service. All of the 46 rooms include gas fireplaces, Jacuzzis, VCRs, and stunning furnishings; however, the deck rooms on the third floor are best. A full complimentary breakfast is served in the dining room. Come evening, Northwest wines are profiled in the library. Watch the ocean, play the piano, or cozy up to the fireplace in the hotel's Chart Room. Prix-fixe dinners are available to guests on a daily basis. *On the beach, at*

J.P.'s (1116 S Hemlock, (503) 436-0908), connected to the Cannon Beach Hotel, sports a hip attitude. The open kitchen features a very theatrical chef (who manhandles fry pans awash with sherry) and a nice selection of tantalizing preparations. Reportedly, the halibut's first rate.

Matanuska and Pacific; (503) 436-2221 or (800) 633-3466; 2740 S Pacific, Tolovana Park, OR 97145; PO Box 219, Cannon Beach, OR 97110; $$$; AE, DC, DIS, MC, V; checks OK.

THE ARGONAUTA INN ☆

In downtown Cannon Beach, between bustling Hemlock Street and the beach, there are a confusing number of lodging options. The Argonauta, not really an inn but rather a cluster of five well-situated residences, is the best of the bunch. All units come equipped with comfy beds, pleasant furnishings, fireplaces, and color TVs. All but one have a complete kitchen. The lower Lighthouse, a retreat for two, is the best deal. The Beach House, while expensive, is more like a miniature lodge (with a river-rock fireplace, a spacious living room, two sun porches, three bedrooms, and two baths). *Corner of 2nd and Larch; (503) 436-2601; 188 W 2nd, PO Box 3, Cannon Beach, OR 97110; $$; DIS, MC, V; checks OK.*

CANNON BEACH HOTEL ☆

Originally a boardinghouse, the Cannon Beach Hotel is a tidy, nine-room operation with a decidedly European flavor. The rooms are reasonable (especially compared to the pricey motels nearby), and vary from a nicely decorated, one-bed arrangement to a one-bedroom suite with a gas fireplace, spa, and ocean view. All rooms include a light breakfast. Pets are not allowed, and neither is smoking. The adjacent restaurant is called J. P.'s at Cannon Beach. *Corner of Gower and S Hemlock; (503) 436-1392; 1116 S Hemlock, PO Box 943, Cannon Beach, OR 97110; $$; MC, V; checks OK.*

SEA SPRITE MOTEL

This cute, always popular oceanfront motel is a good getaway choice for couples or the family (but no pets). Each of the six small but homey units includes a kitchen and color TV. Most have woodstoves. There are a washer and dryer on the premises, and firewood, beach towels, and blankets are provided. If the Sea Sprite is full, ask about the Hearthstone Inn (nonsmoking), located in Cannon Beach and under the same ownership. *At Nebesna and Oceanfront; (503) 436-2266; PO Box 66, Tolovana Park, OR 97145; $$; MC, V; checks OK.*

Manzanita

Resting mostly on a sandy peninsula with undulating dunes covered in

Shop for wine and local artwork at Manzanita Spirits (60 Laneda; (503) 368-6558).

beach grass, shore pine, and Scotch broom, Manzanita is a lazy but growing community gaining popularity as a coastal getaway for in-the-know urbanites. This tiny town is home to a surprisingly significant number of wealthy entrepreneurs and professionals, windsurfers, and excellent restaurants.

> **Stunning Hikes.** Oswald West State Park (3 miles north of Manzanita on both sides of Highway 101; (503) 238-7488) is unsurpassed for scenic beauty in the Northwest, and laced with trails (suitable for hikers or adventuresome trail runners). A world-class hike begins a half-mile south of the Arch Cape tunnel on the west side of the highway. It proceeds 5 miles over Cape Falcon to Short Sands Beach, a picture-perfect cove with a waterfall and steep forested hillsides extending down to water level. Eventually, the trail crosses the highway and heads up to the 1,600-foot summit of Neahkahnie Mountain, the north coast's finest oceanfront panorama. The view from the top of Neahkahnie Mountain (2 switchbacked miles from trailhead to summit) is truly remarkable.

> Oswald West's camping area (the most secluded on the north coast; no

Janice Hondorp, graphic artist and designer, says her favorite hike is the Neahkahnie Mountain trail: "It takes me into a different world." Her favorite mountain biking in the Coast Range includes the grueling ride to the top of Angora Peak, which is about 5 miles northeast of Manzanita.

reservations accepted) is situated a half-mile down a paved trail from the parking area adjacent to Highway 101, where wheelbarrows are available to transport your gear.

> Locals check in regularly at Manzanita News and Espresso (500 Laneda; (503) 368-7450) for the relaxed ambience, the baked goodies, and, of course, a jolt of espresso.

> The Blaze Gallery (220 Laneda; (503) 368-7585; with a location in Cannon Beach) has a selection of Native American art. Also check out the Osborne Gallery (635 Manzanita; (503) 368-7518; very limited hours), featuring many of the owner's paintings. Nehalem's Three Village Gallery (35995 Highway 101; (503) 368-6924) exhibits sculpture, masks, pins, and a collection of decoys.

> You'll find kicked-back, small-town atmosphere at Manzanita Sand-Dune Tavern (127 Laneda; (503) 368-5080), offering pool tables, a gigantic river-rock fireplace, and a motley assortment of disenchanted yuppies and other local characters.

> **Board Heads.** Manzanita's ocean-front and Nehalem Bay have become windsurfing meccas. Learn more at

Manzanita Surf & Sail (150 Laneda; (503) 368-7873), or ask the crew at Cassandra's pizza parlor, the favorite post-"rec" meltdown spot. Board surfers consider the cove at Short Sands Beach (within Oswald West State Park) a favorite spot, particularly in the summer. Long, gnarly rights break at the base of Neahkahnie Mountain, but it's rocky and conditions have to be just right to render it surfable.

 Nehalem Bay State Park (on the south end of Manzanita) offers miles of paved bike paths. Road bikers looking for a long-distance loop head south on Highway 101 to Garibaldi, take the Miami River loop road to Mohler, then return to Highway 101 and Nehalem and Manzanita (approximately 40 rolling miles). Rent bikes at Manzanita Fun Merchants (186 Laneda; (503) 368-6606; with additional locations in Seaside and Cannon Beach).

 If it's flotsam and jetsam you're after, head to the southernmost day-use area of Nehalem Bay State Park (there's a parking fee charged in the summer). Take the short hike over the dune to the beach and head south, to the Nehalem River mouth and jetty.

Fishermen flock to the Nehalem River for salmon and steelhead (particularly the North Fork, which is accessed off Highway 53). The crabbing is good at Nehalem Bay.

 Just south of Manzanita, extending for 4 miles from the north end of Nehalem Bay State Park to the Nehalem River jetty, is one of the better beachcombing stretches in Oregon. The river mouth is home to a vocal – and growing – seal and sea lion population.

Restaurants

JARBOE'S

Jarboe's is in a snug cottage, where the mood is mellow and the food sublime. Menus – which show an imagination – are the work of Danish-born owner/chef Klaus Monberg. His nectarlike crawfish bisque with tender scallops and his simple salad of radishes, endive, filberts, and sun-dried tomatoes prove to be more than the sum of their parts. With Monberg at the grill, simple fresh ingredients take on new textures and flavor. Sauces, like the soups, are light but dynamic. *Laneda and Carmel; (503) 368-5113; 137 Laneda Ave, Manzanita;*

$$$; beer and wine; MC, V; local checks only; dinner Thurs-Mon (Thurs-Sun in winter).

BLUE SKY CAFE

Comfortable but not too casual. Elegant but untraditional (as you'll know right away by the salt and pepper shakers). Seasonal offerings here include such culture-crossing appetizers as delicate sushi served with potted Montrachet and entrées such as spicy Sichuan chicken and roasted stuffed poblano chiles – a delight of colors and tastes. The extensive wine list has an all-Oregon reserve pinot noir section. *Laneda and 2nd; (503) 368-5712; 154 Laneda Ave, Manzanita; $$; full bar; no credit cards; checks OK; dinner Wed-Sun.*

CASSANDRA'S

Now in a new location just a block or so from the pounding Pacific, this pizza parlor cum surfing shrine ensures that you'll be singing "Good Vibrations" in between bites of the best pizza around. Owner and former New Yorker Fawn de Turk assembles ample pies made with fine ingredients. Four can feast on a large primavera – a savory affair built on a base of olive oil, garlic, and herbs with

A couple of miles south of Manzanita, Nina's (Highway 101, Wheeler; (503) 368-6592) serves up hearty marinara-based lunches and dinners. In a reconverted log cabin, Coffee Etcetera (507 Laneda, Manzanita; (503) 368-6030) offers soups, salads, and enchiladas.

mushrooms, green peppers, red onions, and tomatoes, then heaped with provolone, Romano, and mozzarella. The heart of a good pizza is good crust, gobs of cheese, and a zesty sauce, and that's what you'll find here. *Carmel and Laneda; (503) 368-5593; 60 Laneda, Manzanita; $; beer and wine; no credit cards; checks OK; lunch and dinner every day (lunch Sat-Sun only in winter, dinner every day).*

Lodgings

THE INN AT MANZANITA

Unrated

We've yet to return to this place since the new owners bought it, but we hope it is still as subdued and romantic as always. One block off the beach, occupying a multilevel, woodsy setting similar to a Japanese garden, the Inn at Manzanita is a quiet, tranquil retreat. Inside, each of the spacious, nonsmoking units is finished in pine or cedar, with panels of stained glass here and there. All rooms have a gas fireplace, a good-sized spa, a view deck, and a TV with VCR. We remember terrycloth robes and the morning paper at our doorstep and hope the new owners don't forget about all those extra touches. *One block from*

the beach at 67 Laneda; (503) 368-6754;
PO Box 243, Manzanita, OR 97130;
$$$; MC, V; checks OK.

Garibaldi and Bay City

This is Tillamook County, home to four bays: Nehalem, Tillamook, Netarts, and Nestucca. Tillamook Bay – which fronts Garibaldi and Bay City – is the largest and most accessible, and one of the seasonal homes for the summer salmon fleet – or what's left of it, pending ever-increasing government restrictions on commercial fishing. The towns are reaching out for more tourist business to supplement their traditional, but diminishing, logging and fishing income.

▶ Trophy Fish. The Ghost's Hole section of Tillamook Bay, halfway between Garibaldi and Bay City, routinely yields 30-plus-pound Chinook salmon. The Kilchis River, just south of Bay City, is another trophy salmon stream. Barview County Park (off Highway 101 at Barview, just north of Garibaldi) affords excellent jetty fishing. The Miami River (at Garibaldi's south end) is a noted trout stream. Garibaldi Marina (302 Mooring Basin Road, Garibaldi;

Residents swear by the homemade pies at Garibaldi's Diss-L-Dew Diner (1004 Garibaldi; (503) 322-3551).

(503) 322-3312) rents boats and equipment, sells bait, and provides information.

 For fresh seafood, head to Miller Seafood (on Highway 101; (503) 322-0355) or Smith's Pacific Shrimp Company (608 Commercial; (503) 322-3316), both in Garibaldi.

  Bay City's Artspace (9120 Fifth; (503) 377-2783), located in a converted meat market, features unusual avant-garde art and a limited-hours restaurant with dynamite grilled oysters and a great outside deck. Ask here for advice on where to buy the freshest oysters.

Tillamook and Oceanside

A broad, flat expanse of bottomland created by the confluence of three rivers (the Tillamook, Trask, and Wilson), Tillamook is best known as dairy country. Downtown still looks like a working farm town rather than a tourist town. Eight miles west and quaint as can be, tiny Oceanside is Tillamook's beach resort.

 Things can get cheesy around here, especially on the north end of town, where you'll find the Tillamook County

Cape Lookout, in Cape Meares State Park, is a large jewel in Oregon's park system, with 250 campsites, headland-hugging trails, and a huge stretch of little-used beach.

Creamery Association plant and visitors center (4175 Highway 101 N, Tillamook; (503) 842-4481). The tour is self-guided, but there's not a whole lot to see. Still, the place is almost always crowded. The Blue Heron Cheese Company (2001 Blue Heron Drive, Tillamook; (503) 842-8281), about a mile south, is stocked with a variety of cheeses and other made-in-Oregon munchies. There's also a wine-tasting room for Northwest wines.

▶ Scenic Route. The 22-mile Three Capes Scenic Drive, which begins west of Tillamook, is one of Oregon's most beautiful stretches of coastline. The narrow, winding road skirts the outline of Tillamook Bay, climbs over Cape Meares, and brushes past Oceanside. The route then traverses the shores of Netarts Bay before scaling the steep slope of Cape Lookout. Spectacular ocean vistas fill the drive down the south side of the cape. Back at sea level lies a desertlike landscape of sandy dunes. The road to Pacific City and the route's third cape, Kiwanda, runs through lush, green dairy country.

▶ Migrating Whales. Detour from the Three Capes Scenic Drive into

Even though they have to contend with minimal shoulder space and lung-searing climbs, bicyclists favor the Three Capes loop. Check individual park regulations to see if off-road riding is permitted on cape trails.

Oceanside to the top of Maxwell Mountain (a road leads up) for a stunning vantage point of the Pacific and of migrating gray whales. This is a favored launching spot for hang gliders.

▶ **Scenic Trails.** Cape Meares State Park offers a cliff-skirting section of the Oregon Coast Trail, and a paved jaunt down to the Cape Meares Lighthouse (which is open to the public), from which the view, especially at sunset, is breathtaking. Seals and sea lions frolic on the rock reefs below. Be sure to visit the Octopus Tree, a giant Sitka spruce formerly used as a Native American burial tree. Drive to the crest of Cape Lookout (or hike from sea level) and pick up the 3-mile-long trail to the cape's tip, for an awesome ocean vista from the westernmost headland on the north Oregon coast. Along the way, the trail meanders through primeval forests of stately cedar, Western hemlock, and Sitka spruce. Farther south, Cape Kiwanda is a mass of wave-sculpted sandstone cliffs, sand dunes, and sea-level tide pools.

▶ Sandlake, between Cape Lookout and Pacific City along Three Capes Scenic Drive, is mainly a gas station

Canoeists and kayakers can wet their paddles on either side of the Bayocean Peninsula, which divides Tillamook Bay from the ocean.

and a grange hall. But it's also the gateway to thousands of acres of sandy dunes, where off-road vehicle enthusiasts come to play. You're allowed to drive only in designated areas, and regulations are posted. The Forest Service operates 101 campsites (closed during the winter) at the Sandbeach Campground.

▶ Tillamook Bay and the surrounding countryside provide outstanding angling opportunities. The Wilson, Tillamook, and Trask Rivers are superb salmon and steelhead streams. A popular, easily accessible fishing section of the Tillamook River is located adjacent to a state wayside area (with restrooms), 3 miles south of Tillamook just off Highway 101.

▶ Beaver, a logging hamlet 15 miles south of Tillamook along Highway 101, is the jump-off point for the Upper Nestucca River Recreation Area and several Forest Service campgrounds. Adventuresome travelers can drive (or bike) 51 miles, all the way to Willamina, on the western edge of the Willamette Valley. The mostly paved road follows the Nestucca River upstream through old-growth remnant forests, and sees very little traffic.

The Tillamook Naval Air Station Museum (off Highway 101 south of town; (503) 842-1130) has an excellent World War II plane collection, which is housed in one of the world's largest wooden, clear-span buildings, a former blimp hangar.

Restaurants

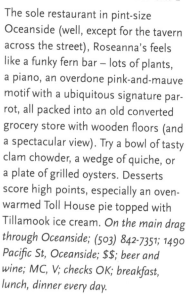

ROSEANNA'S OCEANSIDE CAFE

The sole restaurant in pint-size Oceanside (well, except for the tavern across the street), Roseanna's feels like a funky fern bar — lots of plants, a piano, an overdone pink-and-mauve motif with a ubiquitous signature parrot, all packed into an old converted grocery store with wooden floors (and a spectacular view). Try a bowl of tasty clam chowder, a wedge of quiche, or a plate of grilled oysters. Desserts score high points, especially an oven-warmed Toll House pie topped with Tillamook ice cream. *On the main drag through Oceanside; (503) 842-7351; 1490 Pacific St, Oceanside; $$; beer and wine; MC, V; checks OK; breakfast, lunch, dinner every day.*

Lodgings

HOUSE ON THE HILL

Bring your binoculars. The setting here, on a bluff overlooking Three Arch Rocks (a bird, seal, and sea lion sanctuary) and the blue Pacific, is unbeatable. The house is actually four buildings, home to 16 remodeled units and a honeymoon suite. The Rock Room, with telescopes to spy on the wildlife and scan the horizon for whales, is open to all guests. Choose a unit with a kitchen and stock up on groceries in Tillamook. Kids are fine here. *Maxwell Mountain Rd at Maxwell Point; (503) 842-6030; PO Box 187, Oceanside, OR 97134; $$; MC, V; no checks.*

Cloverdale and Pacific City

Three Capes Scenic Drive rejoins Highway 101 just outside Pacific City, home of the dory fleet (Oregon's oceangoing salmon-fishing boats, which are launched from the beach at Cape Kiwanda). Cloverdale, a dairy community tucked into the lush Nestucca River valley, is a couple of miles north on Highway 101.

> There's always a crowd of view-seekers at Cape Kiwanda, but if it's solitude you're after, head north a couple of miles (on Three Capes Scenic Drive) to the cliffside turnout just north of the tiny beach community of Tierra del Mar. You just might have the spot – and the beach below – to yourself.

> **River Angling.** More salmon and steelhead are taken from the Nestucca

"I've driven all the way south through California to the Mexican border, and I still think that there's nothing more beautiful than driving down the Oregon Coast."

– Carol Johnson, Hebo Ranger District

On the weather in Pacific City: "I don't think I'll ever dry out. The average rainfall here is about 90 inches, and when it snows here on the beach, I get insulted. When I want snow I'll go to it, it does not need to come to me."

– Carol Johnson, Hebo Ranger District

River than any comparatively sized stream in Oregon. The river's accessible from Highway 101 between Beaver and Pacific City. The Little Nestucca River, south of Pacific City and accessible from a secondary road that parallels the river, is another excellent angling prospect.

 Sea kayakers paddle into the Pacific in the lee of Cape Kiwanda (the same route the dories take) to begin a good wave workout.

 Cape Kiwanda offers myriad hiking opportunities, all of them sandy. Park at the adjacent Cape Kiwanda State Park (day-use only) and head on up the sandy slopes. Watch out for hang gliders swooping off the cape from above.

 Robert Straub State Park is situated at the south end of Pacific City and occupies most of the Nestucca beach sand spit, an excellent beachcombing locale.

 Hebo Lake, nestled at the 1,700-foot level of Mount Hebo, is a secluded forest paradise (which gets a lot of winter moisture). There's a campground, a fishing dock, and a reconstructed pioneer shelter. Hebo Lake is 5 miles from Hebo (along

The view from the top of Mount Hebo (elevation about 3,100), a couple of miles up the road from Hebo Lake, is singular; Hebo Ranger District, 31525 Highway 22, PO Box 325, Hebo, OR 97122; (503) 392-3161.

Highway 101, 2 miles north of Cloverdale), on paved Forest Service Road 14. Trails lead into primitive sections of the Coast Range.

Restaurants

GRATEFUL BREAD BAKERY

Transplanted New Yorkers Laura and Gary Seide purvey robust breads, muffins, and a scrumptious array of sweets — carrot cake and gargantuan cinnamon rolls, to name two — in a cheerful, beachy setting. There are breakfast and lunch menus listing some very cheesy New York–style pizza, veggie lasagne, and a few hearty soups. Enjoy your coffee and cake out on the deck. *On the Pacific City loop road; (503) 965-7337; 34805 Brooten Rd, Pacific City; $; no alcohol; MC, V; checks OK; breakfast, lunch every day (closed Jan).*

RIVERHOUSE RESTAURANT

You might see a great blue heron perched on a log on the Nestucca River, which flows idly to the sea right outside the window. The Riverhouse is a calming stop, 3 miles off Highway 101, and far removed from the typical tourist trappings. It's small — 10 or so tables — with hanging plants and a

Stop by Pacific City Seafood (34400 Brooten Road, Pacific City; (503) 965-6687) for fresh seafood and cooked crab.

piano in the corner for local musicians who perform on weekends. Everything's homemade. Don't miss the apple pie. *1/4 mile north of the stoplight on Brooten Rd; (503) 965-6722; 34450 Brooten Rd, Pacific City; $$; full bar; MC, V; checks OK; lunch, dinner every day (days vary in winter).*

Lodgings

HUDSON HOUSE BED AND BREAKFAST

 ☆☆

Perched on a bluff in the middle of nowhere, the picturesque Hudson House evokes memories of a country weekend at Grandma's house. The entire restored Victorian farmhouse is dedicated to the guests; your hosts, the amicable Kulju family, reside next door. The four guest rooms are decorated in an early-century country style and overlook forested hillsides surrounding the pastoral Nestucca River valley. Breakfasts are exceptional, including unusual treats such as British bangers (sausages), Dutch pancakes, and homemade Wholly Cow cereal. *2 1/2 miles south of Cloverdale and east of Pacific City; (503) 392-3533; 37700 Hwy 101 S, Cloverdale, OR 97112; $$; AE, DIS, MC, V; checks OK.*

Blue-shingled with white trim, and a little off the beaten path, the Anchorage is a blue-collar kind of place. There's no luxury here, just quiet and clean accommodations. You're 3 blocks from the Nestucca River estuary and 4 blocks from the ocean, but you can see neither from your $35 room. *6585 Pacific Ave; (503) 965-6773; PO Box 626, Pacific City, OR 97135; $; MC, V; checks OK.*

Neskowin and Otis

Neskowin is a diminutive, mostly residential community lying in the lee of Cascade Head – a steeply sloped and forested promontory. Neskowin affords the final refuge before the touristy "20 miracle miles" (as the stretch from Lincoln City to Newport was formerly called). The beach here is narrower, but decidedly less crowded, than other locales.

⏩ Rain Forests and Meadows.

Majestic Cascade Head has miles of lonely hiking trails that traverse rain forests and meadows, then skirt rocky cliffs with breathtaking vistas. They begin at a marked trailhead about 2 miles south of Neskowin (visible from

Neskowin's Proposal Rock, a little private island in the Pacific, is reachable (at very low tides) from the mainland beach. Be certain to allow for lots of low-tide beach for your return – and don't forget the engagement ring.

Highway 101). Forest Service Road 1861, also called Cascade Head Road (which intersects Highway 101 at the top of Cascade Head), leads to the Harts Cove Trail.

 The Sitka Center for Art and Ecology (on Three Rocks Road, off Highway 101, Neskowin; (503) 994-5485) operates on the south side of Cascade Head and offers summer classes on many subjects, plus numerous talks and exhibits.

 The Neskowin Scenic Route, an enchanting alternative to Highway 101, winds through horse farms and old-growth forests before rejoining the main road at Otis (a couple of miles east of Highway 101). The route is narrow, with lots of climbing and switchbacks. Mountain bikers can climb to the top of Cascade Head on Cascade Head Road (Forest Service Road 1861).

Kayakers and canoeists put in at the boat ramp off Three Rocks Road in the Salmon River estuary.

Restaurants

OTIS CAFE

The Otis Cafe is simply *thriving*. It does all those things small-town

The Salmon River is a
favorite salmon and
steelhead stream.

eateries all over America used to do,
only better – honest, no-frills food at
old-fashioned prices. Everyone appre-
ciates this basic ethic, and on summer
weekends they line up outside for it.
Inside, contented diners nosh on
beefy burgers, thick 'n' chunky soups,
filling breakfasts, and huge milk
shakes. Dinner offerings include fish,
pork chops, and chicken-fried steak.
The buttery black bread is also sold to
go, in case you can't get enough of it
while you're there. *Otis Junction; (503)
994-2813; Hwy 18, Otis; $; beer and
wine; DIS, MC, V; checks OK; breakfast,
lunch every day, dinner Thurs-Sun.*

Lodgings

THE CHELAN

This attractive white-and-blue adobe
structure encompasses nine condo-
minium units, all with lovely ocean
views. There's a manicured front lawn,
lush gardens, and a secluded atmosphere. All the condos have a well-
equipped kitchen, a large living room
with picture window, and a brick fireplace. Upstairs accommodations
(off-limits to children) enjoy private
balconies. *Off Salem Blvd at 48750
Breakers Blvd; (503) 392-3270; PO Box*

The Hawk Creek Cafe (4505 Salem, Neskowin; (503) 392–3838) is your best bet for a beer or a glass of wine, as well as an outdoor deck with a great view.

732, Neskowin, OR 97149; $$$; MC, V; checks OK.

PACIFIC SANDS

A stone's throw from breaking waves, this well-maintained resort condo-motel with an average, bland exterior enjoys a spectacular setting. Only 10 of the condos are for rent; each has a fireplace, kitchen, and more than enough room to stretch out and get comfortable. Opt for a beachfront unit (if available), and step out to miles of untrampled sand and primitive Cascade Head a short distance to the south. *Breakers Blvd and Amity at 48250 Breakers Blvd; (503) 392-3101; PO Box 356, Neskowin, OR 97149; $$; MC, V; checks OK.*

Lincoln City

There is no off-season here. Every weekend is crowded, and traffic can be the pits. Highway 101 just wasn't designed for so many vehicles, and the congestion has local and Oregon Department of Transportation officials helplessly throwing their hands in the air. A slew of factory outlet stores (more than 50 at last count) located halfway through town has created additional gridlock. However, with

Catch the Wind Kite Shop (266 SE Highway 101; (503) 994-9500) is the headquarters for a kite manufacturing company, with eight outlets along the coast.

more people comes more opportunity. In fact, today Lincoln City offers more tourist accommodations than any other Oregon Coast city (and a high percentage of ocean-view rooms).

> **Kite Flying.** As you might expect in a beach town, kite flying is a popular pastime, and so are festivals celebrating the activity. There's a spring kite festival in May, a stunt kite version in July, and an international kite festival in October; Lincoln City Visitor & Convention Bureau, 801 SW Highway 101; (800) 452-2151.

> **Endless Beach.** Beginning at Roads End, a state wayside allows parking and beach access on the north end of town. There are 7 miles of continuous sandy beach for hiking, running, and beachcombing, all the way to Siletz Bay. Throughout the Lincoln City area, numerous streets (which intersect Highway 101) offer beach access. Most offer limited parking.

> **Hang 10, Too.** The Roads End area (on Lincoln City's north side) and the Nelscott area (on the south side, below the Inn at Spanish Head) offer surfing potential. Stop at the Oregon Surf Shop (4933 SW Highway 101; (503) 996-3957), which houses the largest board inventory in the state.

Local Arts & Crafts. The Ryan Gallery, on the north side of town (4270 NE Highway 101; (503) 994-5391), offers an eclectic artwork collection. Mossy Creek Pottery in Kernville, just south of Lincoln City (a half-mile up Immonen Road; (503) 996-2415), sells some of the area's best locally made high-fired stoneware and porcelain.

Devil's Lake (the site of a state park) is stocked with trout and also offers bass, catfish, and perch. The Siletz River is a salmon, steelhead, and trout stream. Surf fishing is popular along the beaches of the Siletz River estuary.

Short, little-known side trips (both south of town) will recharge your spirits after enduring Lincoln City's commercial blitz. The Drift Creek covered bridge is reached via Drift Creek Road (a half-mile south of the city limits off Highway 101). A little way south lies the Kernville junction and Highway 229. Take this road less than a half-mile for a view of the restored Victorian house used in the movie set for *Sometimes a Great Notion*.

Smack dab in the midst of all the hubbub, Cafe Roma (1437 NW High-

Why not head to the source? The ambience isn't that enticing (right in the middle of a strip mall), but the Lighthouse Brewpub (4157 N Highway 101; (503) 994-7238) hand-crafts some alluring ales and offers as many as 25 beers on tap.

way 101; (503) 994-6616) offers a sane haven with coffee drinks, Italian sodas, snacks, and reading material.

Restaurants

THE BAY HOUSE

Shoreside restaurants with spec-tacular views often can get away with serving overpriced, mediocre food. Happily, this is not the case at the Bay House, on the banks of Siletz Bay. The ambience inside is traditional – crisp tablecloths and lots of richly finished wood and brass. The seasonal menu features mostly seafood, sometimes in imaginative preparations such as a grilled catch-of-the-day with shiitake and oyster mushrooms and Bordeaux sauce, along with a blue-cheese potato pancake. Oysters, scallops, crab legs – they're all afforded reverential treat-ment at the hands of chef William Prude. So, too, a rack of lamb. Time your reservations with sunset and ex-perience the solace of Siletz Bay. *5911 Highway 101, on the south edge of town; (503) 996-3222; PO Box 847, Lincoln City; $$$; full bar; AE, DIS, MC, V; checks OK; dinner every day (Wed-Sun in winter).*

DORY COVE

Appreciative crowds continue to flock

There are two state parks, two waysides, and 10 city parks, all within the city limits. On the south end of town, pull into Siletz Bay Park for a sunset picnic.

to this place, rain or shine. Hearty Americana, Oregon Coast–style, is the theme here: lots of seafood, steak, tasty chowder, and 20-plus kinds of burgers (including a half-pound monster). Dessert centers on homemade pie à la mode. Road's End Wayside, a small beachside state park, is right next door. *Next to state park; (503) 994-5180; 5819 N Logan Rd, Lincoln City; $; beer and wine; MC, V; checks OK; lunch, dinner every day.*

CHAMELEON CAFE

Unrated

Lincoln City locals tell us this new little storefront cafe is as delightfully surprising as the critter for which it's named. The meat-and-potatoes crowd can stay home while Chameleon-dwellers dine on the likes of salmon cakes with yogurt and garlic sauce, fish tacos with black beans and rice, and offerings from the Middle East, Greece, and Italy. *On Highway 101; (503) 994-8422; 2145 NW Highway 101, Lincoln City; $; beer and wine; MC, V; checks OK; lunch, dinner Mon-Sat.*

SALMON RIVER CAFE

Unrated

Word is, the newly opened Salmon River Cafe (one part deli and one part bistro) is the place for picnic food. If

Roads End is a good clamming spot; tide tables are available at the nearby Dory Cove.

Tex-Mex? Try Hobie's Adobe (428 SE Highway 101, (503) 994-4419).

you're lucky enough to cadge one of the few tables, you may enjoy service as warm and comforting as the scents wafting from chef Barbara Lowry's open kitchen (Lowry is late of the venerable Bay House). Breakfast features smoked salmon and scrambled eggs served with rosemary- and garlic-kissed potatoes, lunch offerings include Italian-inspired sandwiches, and dinner might be a fresh fish fillet so good it will make you want to come back again the next morning. *Northwest on Hwy 101; (503) 996-3663; 4079B NW Logan Rd, Lincoln City, 97367; $$; beer and wine; no credit cards; checks OK; breakfast, lunch every day, dinner Wed-Sun.*

Lodgings

PALMER HOUSE

Palmer House is a perfect alternative to Lincoln City's glitzy beachfront lodgings. It's a quarter-mile from the beach, in a woodsy setting. The house, originally John Gray's (the developer of the coast's biggest resort, Salishan), is built in the Northwest regional style with three bright, airy guest rooms. Best pick is the Azalea Room, which has an ocean view. *On Inlet, 1/4 mile north of the D River Wayside; (503) 994-7932; 646 NW Inlet,*

Lincoln City, OR 97367; $$$; MC, V; checks OK.

CAMP WESTWIND

¢

During June, July, and August, Camp Westwind, just south of Cascade Head and 5 miles north of Lincoln City, operates as a YWCA camp. The rest of the year, the 500-acre grounds are available for small or large groups. Small means no more than five in the Wy'East cabin, warmed by a stone fireplace and overlooking the mile or so of private beach; large means more than 40 in the main lodge, where a woodstove and a couple of fireplaces keep the cold at bay. Everyone must bring their own bedding, towels, and food. Don't plan on eating out, because you need to cross the Salmon River via barge just to reach the camp. No cars. *Camp is located at 2353 N Three Rocks Rd, Otis, OR 97368; (503) 223-6281 (ask for camp programs); YWCA, 1111 SW 10th Ave, Portland, OR 97205; $; MC, V; checks OK.*

Gleneden Beach

Restaurants

CHEZ JEANNETTE

★★★

Windows with flower boxes, white-washed brick walls, and an intimate

woodsy setting (as well as two fire-places, usually blazing away in winter) give this establishment the appearance of a French country inn. The food, too, is French, traditionally so: butter and cream are used in abundance, and most entrées are carefully sauced. And, bucking the seafood tradition seen up and down the coast, veal, rack of lamb, duckling, and filet mignon make appearances on the menu. Chez Jeannette is by no means a slouch when it comes to seafood, as Umpqua oysters, mussels in sumptuous cream sauce, and poached salmon with aioli will attest. *1/4 mile south of Salishan Lodge; (503) 764-3434; 7150 Old Hwy 101, Gleneden Beach; $$$; full bar; AE, MC, V; checks OK; dinner every day (Tues-Sat in winter).*

Lodgings

SALISHAN LODGE

☆☆

Salishan, the first and perhaps the biggest resort on the Oregon Coast, can seem stuffy, and there's certainly a sense of exclusivity, but the place *is* special. Sprawled over a thousand acres, Salishan includes 205 guest rooms, arranged in eightplex units nicely dispersed over the lush, green landscape. There's an 18-hole (par 72)

Distances within Salishan are considerable, so specify where you'd like to stay depending on what you want to be near (for example: Spruce, Fairway, Chieftain House South, and Sunset Suite overlook the links; Tennis House is near the courts; and the Blue Heron and Tide units have the best views of Siletz Bay and the ocean).

landscape. There's an 18-hole (par 72) golf course, plus driving range, pro shop, and resident PGA professional. You can swim in an indoor pool, work out in the sizable fitness center, sweat in a sauna, or jog on the trails winding through the 750-acre forest. Kids have their own game room and play area. The focal point is a huge lodge with restaurants, a nightclub, a library, meeting rooms, and a gift shop. The guest units are spacious and tastefully furnished but not extravagant, with brick fireplaces, view balconies, splashes of regional art, and individual covered carports. The beach is a good half-mile away.

The main dining room in the lodge was once the premier gourmet destination on the coast. You might encounter a glorious salmon or halibut entrée, or be disappointed by a dry and tasteless paella. Service can be pretentious and prices are sky-high. The voluminous wine list represents a cellar stocked with 20,000 bottles. *Hwy 101 in Gleneden Beach; (503) 764-3600 or (800) 452-2300; PO Box 118, Gleneden Beach, OR 97388; $$$; AE, DIS, DC, MC, V; checks OK; breakfast, lunch, dinner every day.*

When the fish are biting, all those whale-watching boats have gone fishin'. In addition to Deep Sea Trollers (adjacent to the harbor, (503) 765-2248), try Tradewinds Charters, (503) 765-2345.

Depoe Bay

Once a charming coastal community, Depoe Bay is now mostly an extension of Lincoln City's strip development. Fortunately, some of the original town, including its tiny harbor (billed as the "world's smallest"), remains intact.

▶ **Searching for Spouts.** Downtown Depoe Bay, right on the ocean, is a superb spot for storm- and whale-watching. Spectators can take a "saltwater shower" right along the seawall, courtesy of a blowhole located in the rocky ledge below – which blows regularly during winter sou'westers. When it gets really rough, the Pacific is, seemingly, ready to take over the town.

Depoe Bay bills itself as a whale-watching mecca, and during the gray whale migratory season (December–April), the leviathans may cruise within hailing distance of headlands, at times purposefully scraping off troublesome barnacles against offshore rocks. Watch for them at Boiler Bay Wayside (just north of town along Highway 101), another spectacular storm-watching spot. Or head into whale territory. Deep Sea Trollers (downtown, adjacent to the harbor; (503) 765-2248) is one of several

Gracie's Sea Hag (Highway 101 in downtown Depoe Bay; (503) 765-2734) is an institution around these parts, and a great place to catch up on the local scuttlebutt while downing a beer or mug of grog.

operations offering whale-watching cruises.

 Channel Bookstore (Highway 101, 1 block south of the bridge; (503) 765-2352) is a used-book paradise that features everything from paperback romances to Latin grammar.

 The Harbor Gallery (211 SW Highway 101; (503) 765-3113) houses three floors of art, while the O'Connell Gallery (42 N Highway 101; (503) 765-3331) features environmental art and a great water-level view.

 If there's a surf shop here, there must be some choice waves, right? Find out where at the Rock Reef Surf Shop (646 SE Highway 101, just south of the bridge; (503) 765-2306).

  Scenic Views. Fogarty Creek State Park, 2 miles north of town, has a sheltered beach, well protected from coastal winds. There's an annual summer salmon barbecue held here; (503) 765-2889. Come evening, the dramatic rock formations near the shore at Fogarty Creek nicely frame the sunsets and spew sea spray skyward at high tide. A mile farther north, Boiler Bay State Park offers dramatic cliffside photo ops and a good place to spot whales. The park was named for the

There's a fabulous view from every table at Oceans Apart (177 NW Highway 101; (503) 765-2513). At dusk, order a Hawaiian burger and stay for the daily light show. For a snack, try the Lincoln Beach Bagel Company (3930 Highway 101; (503) 764-3882), a couple of miles north of town.

remains of the *J. Marhoffer*, a small freighter that wrecked here in 1910.

Lodgings

CHANNEL HOUSE

☆

Channel House was among the first of the wave of intimate seaside inns. Spectacularly situated on a cliff overlooking the ocean and Depoe Bay Channel (literally right above the water, since there's no beach below), this place has 12 rooms, all with private baths and ocean views. They're truly special accommodations (if rather spendy), each outfitted with a deck, gas fireplace, spa, and in the morning, a breakfast that's aimed to satisfy anyone's hunger. Be sure to bring your binoculars, especially during whale-watching season. *35 Ellingson St, at the end of the street; (503) 765-2140 or (800) 447-2140; PO Box 56, Depoe Bay, OR 97341; $$$; DIS, MC, V; checks OK.*

INN AT OTTER CREST

☆

This rambling destination resort perched on 100 acres at Cape Foulweather is lushly landscaped with evergreens, coastal shrubs, and every color of rhododendron imaginable. Breathtaking views abound, and an isolated low-tide beach awaits, 50 feet below. However, paradise it is not, exactly. For starters, Cape Foulweather is aptly named, as fog often enshrouds the headland. The resort hosts many conventions, which can be intrusive. And it's so large (more than 280 rooms and suites) that it lacks a personal touch (so large, you leave your car a short distance away and hop a shuttle van to your room). Still, most of the rooms, graced with a fireplace, open onto marvelous views. *Otter Crest Loop, 2 miles south of Depoe Bay; (503) 765-2111 or (800) 452-2101; PO Box 50, Otter Rock, OR 97369; $$$; AE, DC, DIS, MC, V; checks OK.*

Newport

The most popular tourist destination on the Oregon Coast, Newport exhibits a blend of tasteful development (the Performing Arts Center, for example) with unending shopping center sprawl. The population is an eclectic mix, including crusty fishermen, artists, retirees, refuge-seeking yuppies, and counter-culturists who never grew up. There's a wealth of variety in Newport; veer off Highway 101's commercial chaos and discover what's here. The Nye Beach area, on the ocean side of Highway 101, has

When the ocean's too chilly – which is the case more often than not – there's a year-round, city-operated indoor pool in town (NW 12th; (503) 265-7770).

fewer tourists and more of an arts-community feel.

 The Newport bay front is a working waterfront going full tilt, where fishing boats of all types – trollers, trawlers, shrimpers, and crabbers – berth year-round. Park your vehicle, walk the waterfront, and soak up the salty ambience. For a bird's-eye perspective of boats, bay, and ocean, take a drive (or a walk) through Yaquina Beach State Park, which wraps around the south end of town.

 Gone Fishin'. Many charter boat operators call the Newport bay front home. Like their colleagues in other harbor towns along the coast, these folks lead salmon, bottom-fishing, and whale-watching excursions. Sea Gull Charters (343 SW Bay; (503) 265-7441) and Newport Sportfishing (1000 SE Bay; (503) 265-7558 or (800) 828-8777) are two popular outfits. Beyond Fishing Marine Discovery Tours (345 SW Bay; (503) 265-6200 or (800) 903-2628) offers unusual saltwater excursions.

 Oceanic Arts Center (444 SW Bay; (503) 265-5963) and the Wood Gallery (818 SW Bay; (503) 265-6843) are galleries worth visiting. The former offers jewelry, paintings, pottery, and sculpture; the latter, functional sculpture, woodwork, pottery, and weaving.

 There's plenty of beach to roam in these parts. Good access points include the Agate Beach area, just north of town, and Devil's Punch Bowl State Park, 8 miles north of Newport. Both spots include parking, restrooms, and a trail to the beach. While you're at Devil's Punch Bowl, stop in for soup, espresso, or baked goods at the oceanfront Otter Rock Cafe (845 First; (503) 765-2628).

 The Yaquina Head Outstanding Natural Area, situated at the north side of Agate Beach, is home to a restored lighthouse (Yaquina Light, built in 1873), open to visitors. There are hiking trails and fantastic cliff-front views. The new showcase intertidal area for viewing marine birds, fish, and mammals is wheelchair-accessible and safe for kids; (503) 265-2863.

 Clamming and crabbing can be excellent in Yaquina Bay. Clam shovels and crabbing gear are available for rent at marine shops such as the Embarcadero Dock (on the bay front at 1000 SE Bay; (503) 265-5435), which also rents boats and bicycles.

The Newport Performing Arts Center (777 S Olive; (503) 265-ARTS) is an attractive wooden structure that hosts music, theater, and other events, some of national caliber.

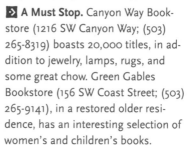 The surf can be up, and honkin', at a number of area breaks. North to south, Devil's Punch Bowl, Beverly Beach, Agate Beach (especially just south of Yaquina Head), and the South Beach area, near the south jetty, all possess superior wave potential.

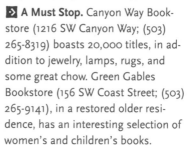 **A Must Stop.** Canyon Way Bookstore (1216 SW Canyon Way; (503) 265-8319) boasts 20,000 titles, in addition to jewelry, lamps, rugs, and some great chow. Green Gables Bookstore (156 SW Coast Street; (503) 265-9141), in a restored older residence, has an interesting selection of women's and children's books.

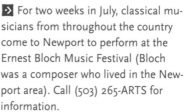 For two weeks in July, classical musicians from throughout the country come to Newport to perform at the Ernest Bloch Music Festival (Bloch was a composer who lived in the Newport area). Call (503) 265-ARTS for information.

 The Newport Visual Arts Center (839 NW Beach; (503) 265-5133) displays traditional and radical art, and offers classes in an oceanfront setting.

 On the south side of the Yaquina Bay Bridge, Oregon State University's Hatfield Marine Science Center (2030

Long known for its chowder and fish 'n' chips, the original Mo's (622 SW Bay; (503) 265–2979) is here. This Mo's offers a lot more of a briny atmosphere than its newer brethren, now scattered up and down the coast.

S Marine Science Drive; (503) 867-0100) offers free marine-life displays, films, and field trips (including whale-watching excursions, which have an admission charge). Look into the summer Seatauqua program.

 The pride of Newport – and the Oregon Coast – is the Oregon Coast Aquarium (2820 SE Ferry Slip Road; (503) 867-3474). It features furry, finny, and feathery creatures cavorting in re-created tide pools, cliffs, and caves. The main attraction is the sea otters; other interesting animals include sea lions, seals, fish native to the Oregon Coast, and seabirds.

 The Newport Seafood and Wine Festival is one of the oldest of its kind and the finest on the coast. Held in late February at the South Beach Marina, (800) 262-7844, it draws from 15,000 to 20,000 people. The festival celebrated its 18th year in 1995.

 Quaff the beer that salty natives drink at the Bayfront Brewery (748 SW Bay; (503) 265-3188), home of the local microbrew, Rogue Ale.

 The area's best, and most extensive, camping area, South Beach State Park, (503) 867-4715, lies a couple of miles south of Yaquina Beach State Park.

Toledo, a mill town located 10 miles inland, is a wonderful side trip for antique and art lovers. Stop in at the Michael Gibbons Gallery (in the Vicarage at 140 NE Alder; (503) 336-2797) and the Main Street Antique Mall (305 N Main; (503) 336-3477).

Head to Yaquina Head (follow the signs to the Outstanding Natural Area) or Cape Foulweather, 9 miles north of Newport (which, unfortunately for sun worshippers, often lives up to its name), to view the sunset.

Restaurants

THE WHALE'S TALE

★★

The Whale's Tale has been purveying the best food in this tourist town inside the bay front's hippest setting for many a year. Customers are a boisterous mix of fishermen, aging hippies, Newport yuppies, and adventuresome tourists who've forsaken Mo's (just down the block). Breakfasts are outstanding: fresh jalapeño omelets, poppyseed pancakes, and home-fried cheese-and-green-chile potatoes. Lunches include good-sized sandwiches, sumptuous soups, and a lusty cioppino. A plate of grilled Yaquina oysters is a dinnertime favorite. Save room for the signature mousse-in-a-bag dessert. *At SW Bay and Fall; (503) 265-8660; 452 SW Bay Blvd, Newport; $$; beer and wine; AE, DC, DIS, MC, V; checks OK; breakfast, lunch, dinner every day.*

CANYON WAY RESTAURANT AND BOOKSTORE

★

Canyon Way is as much an emporium as an eatery, with a bookstore, gift shop, deli, and a restaurant on the premises. You could easily get sidetracked on the way to your table. Stay and you'll find a pleasingly diverse

Good pizza is tough to find on the coast. Try Don Petrie's Italian Food Co. (613 NW Third; (503) 265-3663).

Fish Peddlers Market (617 Bay; (503) 265-7057) is the source for fresh, smoked, and canned seafood.

menu loaded with seafood and fresh pasta plates. A Cajun turkey sandwich, grilled lingcod 'n' chips, and Dungeness crab cakes with angel-hair onion rings are good noontime options. For dinner, there's a different baked oyster preparation daily, and choices as diverse as chicken curry and prawns Provençal. On sunny days, request an outdoor table overlooking the bay. *Between Herbert and Fall Streets; (503) 265-8319; 1216 SW Canyon Way, Newport; $$; full bar; AE, DIS, MC, V; checks OK; lunch Mon-Sat, dinner Tues-Sun (Tues-Sat in winter); bookstore and deli open every day.*

Lodgings

Sylvia Beach Hotel

Owners Goody Cable and Sally Ford have dedicated their pleasantly funky bluff-top hotel to bookworms and their literary heroes and heroines. They gave several like-minded friends the task of decorating each of the 20 rooms, and the results are rich in whimsy and fresh, distinct personality. Most luxurious are the three "classics." The Agatha Christie suite, for instance, is decorated in a lush green English chintz, with a tiled fireplace, a large deck facing out over the sea cliff below, and – best of all – clues from the writer's many murders. The "bestsellers" (views) and the "novels" (nonviews) are quite small, not as impressive, but they are equally imaginative. A mechanized pendulum swings over the Edgar Allan Poe bed; the Cat in the Hat smirks on the wall of the Dr. Seuss room. Books and comfortable chairs abound in the library, where hot wine is served nightly at 10. Breakfast is included in the price of the room. Prepare for a stay sans phones, radios, TVs, and stress.

Dinners in the hotel's Tables of Content restaurant are prix-fixe, reservation-only affairs. The main attraction here is the company; the food gets secondary billing. Each course is brought to your table family-style, making dinner more like a picnic than a gourmet meal. *West on NW 3rd off Hwy 101, 6 blocks to NW Cliff; (503) 265-5428; 267 NW Cliff, Newport, OR 97365; $$; AE, MC, V; checks OK.*

OCEAN HOUSE

If you haven't been here in a while, you'll be surprised. It's bigger, and perhaps not quite as cozy, but hosts Bob and Bette Garrard are still the epitome of congeniality and the setting remains picture-perfect – overlooking the surf at Agate Beach, with Yaquina Head and its lighthouse towering nearby. The four guest rooms are comfortable – neither elegant nor luxurious. There's a small library with cushy chairs and a roaring fireplace in the winter. Outside, you can relax and sunbathe protected from the summer northwest wind (but not from the neighbors) in the sheltered backyard and garden. A short trail leads to the beach below. *Just off Hwy 101 N in Agate Beach (1 block S of Yaquina Head Light House Rd); (503) 265-6158 or (800) 56BANDB; 4920 NW Woody Way, Newport, OR 97365; $$; MC, V; checks OK.*

BROWN SQUIRREL HOSTEL

It's a given that hostels don't offer all the comforts of home. The place can accommodate 22 visitors in five dorm rooms. The proprietor isn't exactly the outgoing type, but hey, you're here for a $10-a-night cheap bunk (bring your own sleeping bag) and the chance to meet like-minded travelers. Private rooms for couples or families fetch $25, and are available only in the off-season (September–June). *Brook and Olive; (503) 265-3729; 44 SW Brook Street, Newport, OR 97365; $; no credit cards; checks OK.*

THE VIKINGS

This place offers some of the sweetest deals on the coast. A collection of 13 rustic cottages sit on an oceanfront bluff, while a steep, but sturdy, staircase leads to an untrampled beach below. The primo bargain, at $55, is #11 with a kitchen, living room, bath, and shower; its romantic, wood-paneled, second-story "crow's nest" features an unbeatable Pacific panorama. *2¹/₂ blocks north of the bridge; (503) 265-2277; 861 S Coast Hwy, Newport, OR 97365; $; AE, DIS, MC, V; no checks.*

Seal Rock

Recently artists and others seeking more elbow room have moved here from crowded Newport. It's still not much more than a patch of strip development along Highway 101, but within that patch are a few keepers, including Yuzen (the best Japanese restaurant along the entire coast) and the 8-acre state wayside at Driftwood Beach along Highway 101 (one of the best views).

▶ Beaver Creek winds its way through Ona Beach State Park (a mile north of town), providing fishing, swimming, and bird-watching possibilities.

If your sweet tooth starts to act up as you drive along Highway 101 near Seal Rock, a stop at the tiny storefront with a sign proclaiming "Fudge," (503) 563-2766, will cure what ails you with a variety of light and dark fudge and good ice cream.

A footbridge takes you to a little-used beach. On the south end of Seal Rock, a state park of the same name features a rocky intertidal area perfect for viewing (look, but don't touch!) starfish, sea anemones, and other marine life.

 Some interesting chain saw art is being created at Seal Rock Woodworks (along Highway 101; (503) 563-2452). Art on the Rocks (5667 NW Pacific Coast Highway, 2 miles north of the Alsea Bay Bridge; (503) 563-3920) has paintings, carvings, crafts, and jewelry.

 Antiques Etc. (Highway 101; (503) 563-2242) is the place to find turn-of-the-century books and even older sheet music — especially for big band–era tunes.

Restaurants

YUZEN

You may think you're hallucinating. A Japanese restaurant in a Bavarian-style building, located in Seal Rock, a blink of a town with a wild West, chain saw-art kind of motif? Wake up. Yuzen purveys the coast's finest Japanese cuisine. You can try everything from a miniature *maki* (tuna) cucumber roll, to *tamago* (egg) and sushi pizza at the sushi bar. Dinners include a decent miso soup and a small salad. Sukiyaki is splendid, as are the tempura dishes. There's even a wafu steak, a traditional Japanese grilled New York steak with veggies. *8 miles south of Newport on Hwy 101; (503) 563-4766; PO Box 411, Seal Rock; $$; beer and wine; MC, V; checks OK; lunch, dinner Tues-Sun.*

Waldport

Take the scenic 9-mile drive east of Waldport to the Kozy Kove (9464 Alsea Highway 34, Tidewater; (503) 528-3251), a restaurant and lounge afloat on the Alsea River.

Small, quiet, unpretentious Waldport is situated on the wide Alsea River estuary, where Highway 101 makes a big bend to accommodate its sandy shore. There are untrampled beaches at either end of town, and a city center unspoiled by schlock.

▶ Waldport is the home of *Inkfish Magazine,* the best source of information for central coast happenings.

▶ Clamming and crabbing are excellent in Alsea Bay. The Dock of the Bay Marina (1245 Mill; (503) 563-2003) rents all you'll need, including boats.

▶ Surf-casting and rock fishing are popular at the west end of Alsea Bay. The Alsea River, home to salmon, steelhead, and sea-run cutthroat trout, is suitable for virtually any type of angling. The Waldport Salmon Derby is

held each fall. Phone the Chamber of
Commerce, (503) 563-2133, for dates
and information.

 Tillicum Beach Campground, operated by the Forest Service, is 4 miles
south of Waldport along Highway 101.
It's a perfect picnic spot with beach
access.

 Park yourself on Yaquina John
Point, at the end of Adahi Road (just
south of town and adjacent to the Cliff
House Bed and Breakfast). There's a
breathtaking view of bay and ocean,
complete with barking seals.

 One of the pristine stretches of the
Coast Range, the remote, pocket-sized
Drift Creek Wilderness, accessible only
by foot or on horseback, is tucked into
the range halfway between Seal Rock
and Waldport; Waldport Ranger District, 1049 SW Pacific Coast Highway;
(503) 563-3211.

Lodgings

CLIFF HOUSE BED AND
BREAKFAST

Unrated

It seems things have gone a bit awry
at this once whimsical retreat. We've
been shocked to hear numerous com-
plaints about the cleanliness and the
service at this place we once called a

Stop for a jolt at
Bumps and Grinds
Coffeehouse (225
Maple; (503) 563-
5769), or browse
through the selec-
tion at Blue Iris
Books (195 Maple;
(503) 563-5488).

dream romantic getaway. We do know the house is exactly where it claims to be — perched on a cliff atop what must surely be one of the Oregon Coast's most prized vistas. Seals and salmon-hungry sea lions frequent the mouth of the Alsea River, and migrating whales pass across the watery panorama of the Pacific. The Bridal Suite houses a tufted velvet sleigh bed with canopy, an oceanfront mirrored bath with Jacuzzi, and a shower for two. Out back, there's an ocean-view deck with Jacuzzi and a hammock for two. However, we're withholding our star rating until things settle down and we can fully re-review. *1 block west of Hwy 101 on Adahi Rd; (503) 563-2506; PO Box 436, Waldport, OR 97394; $$$; MC, V; checks OK.*

Yachats

Yachats (pronounced yah-hots) takes its name from a Chinook Indian word meaning "dark waters at the foot of the mountain," which fits this small community's setting, on a narrow basaltic terrace straddling the Yachats River. Paths lead down from seaside bluffs to beaches and rocky tide pools at the state park and across the river mouth at Yachats Ocean Wayside.

From May to September, tasty, sardinelike smelt follow the call of the high tides to spawn on the sandy shores here. Locals, armed with small dipnets, scoop them out of the surf. Several hundred pounds of them are cooked up at the mid-July Smelt Fry, held at Yachats Commons.

▶ **Trails with a View.** The 2.6-mile roundtrip St. Perpetua Trail (which begins at the Cape Perpetua Visitors Center) climbs 600 feet to the West Shelter, a stone hut on the brow of the cape that on a clear day takes in an extraordinary 150-mile panorama up and down the coast, from Cape Foulweather down to Cape Blanco. It's also a fine eyrie for spying whales passing far below. There are numerous other trails (shorter and longer), and the visitors center (2400 Highway 101 S; (503) 547-3289), where trail maps are available, is a good starting point. Those in search of a tamer hike should head for the Yachats 804 Trail, which begins at the Smelt Sands Wayside at the north end of town and winds its way along the ocean bluffs.

This is national forest territory, crisscrossed with hiking trails that lead to isolated coves. The driftwood-strewn beaches and rocky ledges are often bombarded by monstrous ocean waves. Other paths head deep into bona fide rain forest (with 400 tons of plant life per acre) and into the Cummins Creek Wilderness Area. Cape Perpetua is one of the wettest regions on the Oregon Coast; the cape's summit gets well over 100

South of Yachats, the 2,780-acre Cape Perpetua Scenic Area embraces one of the most spectacular sections of the Siuslaw National Forest. The namesake cape, a prominent basaltic headland, towers 800 feet over the coast. At the foot of the cape, heavily visited Devil's Churn is a narrow fissure where frothing seawater surges in and out.

inches of rain annually. If you hike the trails, particularly in the backcountry, bring rain gear; even when it's clear and sunny to the north or south, you may see moisture here.

 A half-mile south of Cape Perpetua is Strawberry Hill, an easily missed picnic area where wild strawberry plants flower in the spring. Throughout the year, harbor seals lounge like plump gray slugs on the rock shelf 30 yards offshore. April, May, and June are the prime months to look for their newborn pups, which weigh about 20 pounds. The rocky coastal fringe here forms some of the best tide pools, alive with swaying sea anemones, sea urchins, scuttling hermit crabs, periwinkles, and a miniature world of other intertidal sea organisms. Up above, spectacular headlands afford ocean-viewing or whale-watching promontories.

 The Yachats River Road (turn at the bridge) is a little-used paved route that heads into an undeveloped area of the Coast Range. Trail riders should pick up a map of the Cummins Vista mountain bike loop from the Cape Perpetua Visitors Center.

 The next large headland to the south is Heceta Head, named for

For fine views, drive the aptly named Auto Tour Viewpoint Road (off Highway 101, 3 miles south of Yachats), a switch-backed blacktop that winds its way up Cape Perpetua. Trails leading from the parking area on top provide sweeping vistas.

The colorful Yachats Kite Festival lifts off during blustery October (usually the first Saturday), when the winds grow strong enough to float kites as big as Oldsmobiles; (503) 547-3530.

18th-century Spanish navigator Bruno Heceta. Heceta Head Lighthouse is the Oregon Coast's most powerful – and popular – beacon. The darling of lighthouse buffs, it's said to be the most photographed on the West Coast; however, it's not open to the public. From April through August, look for colonies of Brandt's cormorants, which nest on the rugged south slope.

▶ Though at first they appear on the highway like a misplaced Disney sideshow, the Sea Lions Caves (91560 Highway 101; (503) 547-3111; $5.50 per adult), 11 miles north of Florence, are nevertheless one of the central coast's most impressive natural phenomena, the only place on the U.S. mainland where Steller's sea lions can be seen year-round. And it's much less kitschy than all the advance hype might suggest. (Can 200,000 visitors a year possibly be wrong?)

An elevator carries you 208 feet down into the vast, surf-swept cavern, where the booming of the waves mingles eerily with the tenor barking of the sea lion bulls. As your eyes adjust to the gloom, you'll see the sea lions frolicking or dozing on the rocks, some within arm's reach. They occupy the

For books, stop in at the Purple Rose Studio (153 Highway 101; (503) 547-3222), a book, music, and card shop.

"You're only an hour away from Eugene. You get all the benefits of living in a small town, with a great city just a short drive away."

– Tom Douglass, assistant manager, Sea Lions Caves

cave during the fall and winter; in spring and summer they give birth to their young just outside the cave.

 Favorite galleries include: Earthworks Gallery (2222 N Highway 101; (503) 547-4300), which exhibits Northwest artists, the Backporch Gallery (Fourth and Highway 101; (503) 547-4500), and the Tole Tree (2334 Highway 101; (503) 547-3608).

Restaurants

LA SERRE

The fine dining choice in Yachats, La Serre ("the greenhouse") is the best restaurant in the culinary poverty zone between Newport and Coos Bay. The main dining area has an airy, open-beamed ceiling with skylights and the largest collection of plants this side of Cape Perpetua's rain forest. The aroma of garlic and saffron drifts down from the open kitchen. Seafood, as befits a seaside town, is a good bet, be it catch-of-the-day Pacific whitefish, Umpqua oysters, or zesty cioppino. *2nd and Beach, downtown Yachats; (503) 547-3420; PO Box 286, Yachats; $$; full bar; AE, MC, V; checks OK; dinner every day, breakfast Sun (closed Tues, Oct-June).*

The lounge at the Adobe Resort (1555 Highway 101; (503) 547-3141) is as ocean-front as you can get. The food's nothing to write home about, but the view is definitely worth the price of a drink or brew.

NEW MORNING COFFEEHOUSE ☆

A cross-section of Yachats society attends the New Morning: tourists, hip locals in Gore-Tex and faded jeans, and Eugene weekenders. Muffins, Danish, pies, and coffeecakes are superb. Savory soups and black bean chili are typical luncheon fare. They are experimenting with Thursday and Friday night pasta dinners, but you'll alway be sure to find a good selection of coffees to enjoy by the homey woodstove – just what a soul needs on a stormy day on the Oregon Coast. *At Hwy 101 and 4th St; (503) 547-3848; 373 Hwy 101 N, Yachats; $; beer and wine; no credit cards; checks OK; breakfast, lunch Wed-Sun.*

Lodgings

SEA QUEST BED AND BREAKFAST

There are few B&Bs on the coast of Oregon better situated (well, the Ziggurat next door, perhaps). At Sea Quest you spend the night in a luxurious, estatelike structure on a sandy bluff right above the ocean and nearby Ten Mile Creek. All five guest rooms have private baths *and* spas, plush queen-size beds, private entrances,

Favorite outdoor spots: Cape Perpetua and Strawberry Hill beach, a little way south, where there are lots of agates and marine life.

– Donald Niskanen, co-owner, New Morning Coffeehouse

and an ocean view. Miles of Pacific vistas from the living room. *6½ miles south of Yachats on west side of Hwy 101 (between mile markers 171 and 172); (503) 547-3782; 95354 Hwy 101, Yachats, OR 97498; $$$; MC, V; checks OK.*

ZIGGURAT

This stunning glass-and-wood four-story structure takes its name from the ancient Sumerian word for "terraced pyramid." The scintillating views from all 40 windows keep most guests occupied, especially during storms; however, there are also plenty of books and board games in the 2,000-square-foot living room. The east suite boasts a sauna, while the west suite has a round, glass-block shower and a magnificent view. Upstairs, at the apex of the pyramid, there's a guest room with open-air decks. *6½ miles south of Yachats on west side of Hwy 101 at 95330 Hwy 101; (503) 547-3925; PO Box 757, Yachats, OR 97498; $$$; no credit cards; checks OK.*

THE ADOBE RESORT

Ensconced in a private, parklike setting, the Adobe fans out around the edge of a basalt-bumpy shore. At high tide, waves crash onto the rocks below while their thunder echoes into the rooms. The original rooms – with beamed ceilings, fireplaces, and ocean views – are quite popular; the two newer wings have more amenities (refrigerators and coffeemakers), but only some have fireplaces and face the ocean. There's a six-person Jacuzzi and a sauna for all. Children are welcome, and some pets. The restaurant is overpriced, yet rates a notch above the usual mediocre oceanfront fare. *In downtown Yachats at 1555 Hwy 101; (503) 547-3141; PO Box 219, Yachats, OR 97498; $$; AE, DC, DIS, MC, V; local checks only; breakfast, lunch Mon-Sat, dinner every day, brunch Sun.*

BURD'S NEST INN BED AND BREAKFAST

This is one distinctive roost, perched halfway up a hillside and enjoying a big bird's-eye view of the Pacific. This half-century-old home has a cluttered but comfortable look, especially inside, where antiques, unusual toys, and knickknacks compete for wall and table space. Proprietors Big Burd and Joni Bicksler, escapees from Southern California, lend an animated, friendly ambience and specialize in big Mexican breakfasts. *East side of Hwy 101, just before the bridge; (503) 547-3683; 664 Yachats River Rd, Yachats, OR 97498; $$; MC, V; no checks.*

Cape Cod Cottages ☆

Cape Cod Cottages, sitting on a low-lying bank just off Highway 101 between Waldport and Yachats, occupy 300 feet of this ocean frontage. There are nine spic-and-span and cozy one- and two-bedroom units. All come with completely equipped kitchens, fireplaces (with wood provided), decks, and picture windows overlooking the ocean. Some even have garages. All in all, a nice, out-of-the-way place where children are welcome. *2¹/₂ miles south of Waldport, on Hwy 101; (503) 563-2106; 4150 SW Pacific Coast Hwy, Waldport, OR 97394; $$; AE, MC, V; checks OK.*

Edgewater Cottages ☆

Lots of honeymooners land here, and the place is usually booked from the beginning of the tourist season. The seven units are varied and rustic-looking, with lots of wood paneling. The cute, pint-size Wheel House (a steal at $35) and Crow's Nest are strictly 2-person affairs, while the Beachcomber can accommodate as many as 15 guests. Every cottage has an ocean view, a fireplace, a kitchen, and a sun deck. There's only one phone on the premises, but other necessities, such as corkscrews and popcorn poppers, are available. Kids and well-behaved dogs are fine (but pets cost extra). *2¹/₂ miles south of Waldport, on Hwy 101; (503) 563-2240; 3978 SW Pacific Coast Hwy, Waldport, OR 97394; $$; no credit cards; checks OK.*

OREGON HOUSE

You can't see Oregon House from the highway, and therein lies its charm. It's definitely private, out of the wind, and away from the hustle and bustle. An interesting complex of five buildings in a woodsy setting. Some of the units have fireplaces, but none have phones or TVs; in some you'll step out on the balcony to enjoy the ocean view, in others you'll relax in a wicker rocking chair or a big brass bed. All have kitchen facilities and most have a view of the ocean. Take the cliffside trail down to the uncrowded beach. Kids are fine. *8 miles south of Yachats on the west side of Hwy 101; (503) 547-3329; 94288 Hwy 101, Yachats, OR 97498; $$; DC, DIS, MC, V; checks OK.*

THE SEE VUE   ¢

Perched cliffside between Cape Perpetua and Heceta Head, the See Vue lives up to its name. Each of the

11 units (most are under $50) in the cedar shake–sided lodging is different. The Salish, done up in a Northwest Indian motif, is an excellent deal. Meander down to the uncrowded beach a few hundred yards away. For a small additional charge you may bring your dog. *6¹/₂ miles south of Yachats on Hwy 101; (503) 547-3227; 95590 Highway 101, Yachats, OR 97498; $; MC, V; checks OK.*

WAYSIDE LODGE ¢

Located a couple of miles north of town, the Wayside is a low-lying, ocean blue structure nestled in a thicket of shore pines and nicely sheltered from Highway 101. There's a grassy area out back just above the beach, and even though houses are situated on either side, a feeling of privacy prevails. The best deal here is the beach-accessible studio. All rentals have kitchens. *2 miles north of Yachats; (503) 547-3450; 5773 N Highway 101, Yachats, OR 97498; $; DIS, MC, V; checks OK.*

Florence

During the last 20 years, the sleepy lumber and fishing port of Florence has reinvented itself as a vibrant

Locals head out South Jetty Road, south of Florence on Highway 101, for miles of broad, sandy beach and pounding surf, plus high dunes zoned for use by off-road vehicles.

tourist mecca. The tastefully revitalized Old Town has become decidedly visitor-oriented – with cafes, gift shops, a movie house concentrated along riverside Bay Street – without succumbing to the schlock that afflicts other parts of the Oregon Coast.

 Miles of Dunes. The real attraction on this stretch of coast is the 53-mile-long Oregon Dunes National Recreation Area, 32,000 acres of mountainous sand dunes, freshwater lakes, beaches, and marsh, to which Florence is the northern gateway. Stretching 40 miles from Florence to North Bend, the extraordinary Oregon Dunes was established by Congress for its scientific and historic value as well as for recreation and conservation. Because from the highway you can only glimpse this sandy wilderness, plan to stop and explore on foot. Good starting points near Florence include the Cleawox Lake area of Honeyman Memorial State Park and the Tahkenitch Lake area a few miles farther south.

 Pitch Your Tent. To camp at the Oregon Dunes (855 Highway Avenue, Reedsport, OR 97467; (503)-271-3611), choose from 14 U.S. Forest Service campgrounds; of these, eight allow off-road vehicles. For reservations,

At the end of South Jetty Road in the Oregon Dunes is a fishing/crabbing pier and the South and North Jetties, which channel the Siuslaw River out to sea. While you fish, watch hundreds of wintering tundra swans, with their 6-foot wingspans, which inhabit the wetlands from mid-November to February.

call (800) 280-2267. The majority are nestled amid the dunes; some are near a river or lake. Tyee River, Carter Lake, and Tahkenitch Lake have boat ramps; Tahkenitch Campground, Eel Creek, and Spinreel offer picnicking; Spinreel and Horsfall have staging areas for off-road vehicles; Driftwood, Taylor, Tahkenitch, Spinreel, and Horsfall are wheelchair-accessible; Spinreel, Wild Mare, and Horsfall have horse-staging lots; and hiking opportunities are plentiful at all. None of the campgrounds have hookups, and a 10-day stay is usually the maximum.

▶ Mush, You Huskies! The Oregon Dunes Mushers Mail Run, held since 1977, is a one-of-a-kind event – a dogsled race with a twist, held not on snowy tundra but across miles of sand dunes and forest trails. The world's longest dry-land run, it spans the length of the dunes from Horsfall Beach in the south to the dunes west of Florence.

Two classes of teams participate, using specially designed four-wheel sleds: mini-teams consist of 3 or 4 dogs and cover 55 miles; traditional teams of 5 to 12 dogs traverse the whole grueling 72 miles. Proceeds from the run, held the second week-

The Old Town Coffee Company (1269 Bay; (503) 997-7300) brews hearty pots of gourmet java and displays works by local artists.

end in March from 7am to dusk, go to support an Oregon competitor in Alaska's famed Iditarod Trail Sled Dog Race. Before the run, you can buy souvenir envelopes commemorating the route at the Florence and North Bend Chambers of Commerce; the envelopes are hand-canceled at the post offices, carried on the sleds during the race, and signed by the driver. Afterward, all the teams gather for a parade and other festivities in Old Town Florence.

Go down to the beach in any of the areas between Florence and Coos Bay; head to Lakeside in the late afternoon Saturday to see the mini-teams, and to Winchester Bay on Sunday morning to see the start of the final stretch. For more information, call the Bay Area Chamber of Commerce at (800) 824-8486 or the Florence Visitors Center at (503) 997-3128.

> **A Sternwheeler Cruise.** The 65-foot *Westward Ho,* a modern replica of an 1850s sternwheeler, moored at the Bay Street dock in Old Town, cruises up the Siuslaw River to Mapleton and back. The Rockin' 'n' Rollin' on the River tour (Saturdays, 1–3pm) includes live music, cards and board games, old-time photos, beer, wine,

The International C-Food Market (1498 Bay; (503) 997-9646) is a spacious, airy restaurant built on pilings over the Siuslaw River. Fishing boats offload their bounty right outside daily; if you want a fresher seafood dinner, you'll have to net it yourself.

and a gourmet salmon brunch ($20 for the cruise; $13 for the brunch; kids under 13 for $10). The Time Warp Cruise (Sundays, 1–3pm) includes a narrated "living history" cruise. Enjoy the complimentary champagne with chicken brunch while taking in the tidal river and wildlife scenery (PO Box 3023, Florence, OR 97439; (503) 997-9691).

> **Botanical Wayside.** The Darling-
tonia Botanical Wayside, just off Highway 101 4 miles north of Florence, protects 18 boggy acres where the unusual carnivorous pitcher plant *(Darlingtonia californica)* thrives. To compensate for the nitrogen-poor wetland soil, the plants feed on insects, which are lured by scent and nectar into the flaring stem. Once inside, the victims become trapped and are eventually digested. The pitcher plants, shaped something like a snake's head (hence another nickname – the cobra lily), bloom in May and June, but can be seen here throughout most of the year; a quarter-mile loop trail leads through the wooded preserve for a close look.

> C&M Stables (90241 Highway 101
N, Florence, OR 97439; (503) 997-7540), 8 miles north of Florence on

Highway 101, offers horseback journeys that let riders of all abilities explore secluded ocean beaches and forests of the Coast Range. Guided beach rides of 1½ ($23) and 2 hours ($28) leave the ranch on a trail winding through scenic dunes and onto the beach; sunset rides last 2 hours. You may even ride all day, if you can. Reservations are highly recommended. Large groups can be accommodated, especially in summer.

Restaurants

BLUE HEN CAFE

Just try to suppress a cackle when you notice the glass, ceramic, and plastic chickens – blue, naturally – everywhere. What's important, though, is that the place is friendly, the prices are reasonable, the food is tasty, and there's lots of it. As you might expect, chicken (mostly fried) dominates the menu. You'd be hard pressed to finish off an entire "four-cluck" special. *On Hwy 101 in the north part of town; (503) 997-3907; 1675 Hwy 101 N, Florence; $; beer and wine; DIS, MC, V; local checks only; breakfast, lunch, dinner every day.*

Lodgings

JOHNSON HOUSE BED AND BREAKFAST

☆☆

We can't recommend *any* hotels in Florence, so we're thankful for the wit, curiosity, and lofty aesthetic standards Jayne and Ron Fraese bring to their perennially popular B&B. Reflecting the Fraeses' interests (he's a political science prof, she's an English teacher), the library is strong on local history, natural history, politics, and collections of essays, letters, cartoons, and poetry. There are six guest rooms, one of which is a cute garden cottage outside, furnished in a way not out of keeping with the 100-year-old house. Breakfasts, which include fresh garden fruit and produce (grown out back) and home-baked bread, are among the best on the coast. In addition, two cabins are spectacularly situated 10 miles north. Calling them breathtaking would be an understatement. *1 block north of the river at 216 Maple St; (503) 997-8000; PO Box 1892, Florence, OR 97439; $$ (cabins $$$); MC, V; checks OK.*

EDWIN K BED AND BREAKFAST

☆

Built in 1914 in the Craftsman style by one of Florence's founders, the Edwin

K is set in a quiet residential neighborhood beyond the bustle of Old Town. Ivory wall-to-wall carpeting contrasts nicely with aged and swarthy Douglas fir woodwork. All four guest rooms are fitted with antiques. On the more modern side, a spacious double shower graces one bath, a whirlpool tub another. Breakfast is served in the formal dining room, another shrine to the woodcrafter's art. *On the west edge of Old Town, across the street from the river at 1155 Bay St; (503) 997-8360 or (800) 8EDWINK; PO Box 2687, Florence, OR 97439; $$; MC, V; checks OK.*

GULL HAVEN LODGE ¢

It's actually closer to Yachats than Florence, and the setting is perhaps as close to perfect as any lodging on the Oregon Coast. A 360-degree panorama is available from Shag's Nest, an isolated, one-room cabin equipped with a fireplace, kitchenette, and private deck (you'll need to book it well in advance). For the bath, you must scamper across to the lodge 30 yards away. The lodge units aren't as good a deal. Minimum-stay requirements apply here year-round. *8 miles south of Yachats; (503) 547-3583; 94770 Highway 101, Florence, OR 97439; $; MC, V; checks OK.*

Reedsport

The faded logging center of Reedsport hasn't yet fully discovered its potential and personality on the 101 stretch, midway between Florence and Coos Bay. But this port town of 5,000 on the Umpqua River is the center for information on the dunes, and the wharf area is undergoing revitalization. The Umpqua itself is renowned among anglers for its spring chinook run and fighting steelhead; shad runs spring and summer, and sturgeon and striped bass are taken from the lower stretches.

 Located wharfside on the Umpqua River, a half-mile east of Highway 101, the Umpqua Discovery Center (409 Riverfront Way, Reedsport, OR 97467; (503) 271-4816 or (800) 247-2155) opened in mid-1993 and features two main exhibits. The "Umpqua Experience" examines the region's human and natural history. The more unexpected "Antarctic Experience" relates the story of antarctic exploration; the main attraction here is the 300-ton, wood-hulled *Hero*, a retired antarctic research vessel that bears the scars of its years of scientific service in the brutal southern seas. Admission to all

Other residents and seasonal visitors at the Dean Creek Elk Viewing Area include western bluebirds, black-tailed deer, ospreys, great blue herons, and mallard ducks. Binoculars will definitely come in handy here.

The well-informed staff makes the Oregon Dunes National Recreation Area Headquarters (855 Highway Ave, Reedsport, OR 97467; (503) 271-3611) a useful stop for tips on hiking trails and on where to go to spot elk, ospreys, and other wildlife.

exhibits is $5 for adults, half that for kids 5 and up.

 Wildlife Viewing. Three miles east of Reedsport, the Dean Creek Elk Viewing Area is a 1,040-acre preserve alongside the Umpqua River. It is a wildlife-rich mosaic of wetlands, pasture, and forest. Top billing, of course, goes to the herd of 60 to 100 Roosevelt elk, the largest species of its kind in the world. Males can weigh in at over 700 pounds, bearing massive racks; females are smaller and lack antlers. Both wear shaggy manes that help distinguish them from deer. The majestic elk are year-round residents, but they're often scarce; they usually emerge from the sheltering woods at dawn and dusk.

Sections of the wetlands have been enhanced to provide more standing water for a variety of wildlife. Canada geese winter here and nest on the pastures. Along streambanks and marsh edges, look for nutria, dog-size rodents that resemble beavers, but with a ratlike tail. Introduced from South America around 1900 for the fur market, the nutria quickly adapted – too well – and rapidly spread throughout much of the United States. Keep your eyes open for less conspicuous creatures, too: rough-skinned newts, garter snakes, frogs, and other reptiles and amphibians. For more information, contact the Bureau of Land Management (1300 Airport Lane, North Bend, OR 97459; (503) 756-0100) or stop by the National Recreation Area information center in Reedsport.

Winchester Bay

Four miles southwest of Reedsport down Highway 101 at Winchester Bay is the Salmon Harbor Marina and its thicket of commercial and private boats; with nearly a thousand slips, this is the largest sport-fishing marina on the Oregon Coast.

> **Lake Fishing.** Tenmile and North Tenmile Lakes, interconnected twin lakes formed when Coast Range streams were dammed by sand dunes, attract anglers (for bluegill and largemouth bass), swimmers, water-skiers, and canoeists, who can explore the many arms. Located east of Lakeside (Rte. 101) and northeast of Oregon Dunes National Recreation Area.

> Spinreel Dune Buggy Rentals (9122 Wildwood Drive, North Bend, OR 97459; (503) 759-3313), about 2 miles south of Tenmile Lakes (look for mile

marker 224), rents Odyssey dune buggies ($30 per hour, $155 all day) and other off-road vehicles, including miniature four-wheelers for kids. You can take a spin along the beach or putter up and down the dunes. Phone ahead in winter.

▶ Thar She Blows! The working Umpqua River Lighthouse, built in 1894, is open to the public by appointment, (503) 440-4500, but its grounds in the Umpqua Lighthouse State Park offer a prime whale-watching perch, 100 feet above sea level, any time. From Alaska's Bering and Chuckchi Seas, pregnant gray whales begin passing the Oregon Coast in late November – usually averaging one whale per hour – on their 12,000-mile maternity run to the warmer waters off Baja California. In late December, the main pulse arrives, when one whale may swim past every two minutes or so. March–May, they make their way north again.

▶ Doing the Dunes. If you've got time for just one jaunt into the dunes, the Umpqua Dunes Trail, an easy, 4-mile round-trip, is a prime candidate, taking you into some of the highest dunes and far from the sputter of off-road vehicles. From Eel Creek

Winchester Bay is a good spot to book a fishing charter; several outfits are based here, including Gee Gee Charters, (503) 271-3152 or (503) 271-4134, which runs bottom-fish and chinook expeditions. And when you return to port, bone tired but full of good stories (and, hopefully, your limit), you'll find several salmon canneries and smokehouses to process your haul.

Campground, 11 miles south of Reedsport, follow the foot trail west. After a quarter-mile climb through a forest of evergreens and rhododendrons, you'll break through the tree line and step out onto some of the most impressive dunes in all of this miniature Sahara, cresting nearly 500 feet high.

After about another mile across the sand, you reach the "deflation plain," a low-lying marshy area that's gradually being reclaimed by pine forest. Deer and other animals can be spotted here, as well as a variety of native plants, including the insectivorous sundew. Follow the blue-banded poles marking the route another three-quarters of a mile to the beach. (A shorter alternative: join ranger-led groups on the Eel Creek Dunes Trail, a 1-mile loop, leaving the Eel Creek Campground Wednesdays at 2pm, late June–August.)

▶ **A Crab Hunt.** One of the more offbeat events on the central coast is the Kleo the Krab Bounty Hunt. This local family favorite runs from mid-August though Labor Day. Several score live crabs are tagged and released into the harbor, then the public is invited to catch them (supplying their own crab

pots and other equipment). Partici-
pants win T-shirts and other prizes.
To the lucky crabber who lands Kleo
goes a hefty $1,000; if Kleo hasn't
been nabbed by Labor Day, a winner is
chosen by lottery. For more details,
call the Lower Umpqua Chamber of
Commerce (PO Box 11, Reedsport, OR
97467; (503) 271-3495 or (800) 247-
2155).

North Bend

Near the southern end of the dune
country, North Bend, Coos Bay, and
Charleston – collectively dubbed the
"bay area" – combine to form the largest urban area on the Oregon Coast.
North Bend began in the mid-1800s
as a company town where sea captain
and shipbuilder Asa Simpson established a sawmill and shipyard. Though
the town was in a rugged coastal fron-
tier, replete with saloons and houses
of ill repute, it was picturesque and
prosperous enough to attract new-
comers as highways and railways were
erected nearby. Today's North Benders
bear a striking resemblance to the
early settlers – a population of solid
working folk, retirees, and the occasional new face.

In mid-March, North Bend and Coos Bay pump up the volume with a three-day jazz festival, held annually since 1988: the South Coast Dixieland Clambake Jazz Festival (PO Box 374, North Bend, OR 97459; (503) 756-4613). More than a dozen bands play at four venues around the area (connected by a shuttle), with a program aimed mainly at an over-40 crowd. Tickets are about $40 for all three days. The Sunday morning gospel service is free.

Restaurants

THE BRASS RAIL

A visual oasis in an otherwise frumpy downtown. On looks alone, the Brass Rail's interior is a must-see. It's a mini-maze of rooms chock-full of stunning antique furniture, stained glass, and skylights. A garden court-yard accommodates outdoor eating in temperate weather. Avoid the attempts at culinary cuteness and order something your mom might have made. *Hwy 101 at the south end of downtown; (503) 756-2121; 2072 Sherman Ave, North Bend; $; beer and wine; AE, DIS, MC, V; checks OK; breakfast Sat–Sun, lunch Mon–Sat.*

Lodgings

HIGHLANDS BED AND BREAKFAST

It's the secluded, woodsy setting and the view of the Coast Range and Coos Bay that lure people to these 6 acres of highlands. Then there's the comfortable 2,000-square-foot lower level of Marilyn and Jim Dow's contemporary cedar home. A commodious living room with a soapstone stove and wraparound windows is at your disposal, as is a private solarium deck with a spa. If you want to try your hand at crabbing, the Dows will loan you their crab ring and cook whatever good creatures you net. No children under 10. *Please call for directions; (503) 756-0300; 608 Ridge Rd, North Bend, OR 97459; $$; MC, V; checks OK.*

Coos Bay

The south bay's port city and formerly the world's foremost wood-products exporter, Coos Bay has been undercut by a sagging timber industry and the political struggle to control the future of the Northwest's forests. But this Scandinavian/German-founded town still has the largest and busiest natural harbor between San Francisco and Seattle.

And that's the impression visitors get as they enter the town along Highway 101 – steaming mills and industrial areas, with few of the bells and whistles that induce highway cruisers to pull over and linger. Much of the downtown's architecture and businesses look unchanged from the 1950s. But frankly, that's part of Coos Bay's rough-around-the-edges charm.

Coos Bay is making the slow transition from a resource-based economy to one that's service-based, and that means catering – albeit grudgingly – to tourism. The downtown wharf area, for example, is being spruced up, with informative displays on Coos Bay's maritime and timber history (including a dry-docked tugboat), and there are even some big-city cultural surprises in store.

▶ Fine Art. Coos Art Museum (235 Anderson Street, Coos Bay, OR 97420; (503) 267-3901) is the biggest surprise in this burly mill town – the only coastal art museum between San Francisco and Vancouver, British Columbia. The centerpiece of local cultural efforts, the museum, with 3,500 square feet of exhibit space, is housed in the art deco former post office building in central downtown.

The impressive permanent collection features American prints, oils, watercolors, and sculpture, and includes works by Larry Rivers, Robert Rauschenberg, and James Rosenquist. The Mabel Hansen Gallery and Oregon Gallery usually spotlight works by up-and-coming artists. One of the most popular annual events is the "Public Hanging," an unjuried exhibit held in autumn showcasing artists from around Oregon. The museum is a venue for dance and music performances, and also sponsors classes and workshops in various art media. The first-floor gift shop carries contemporary art and handcrafts – limited-edition prints, ceramics, jewelry – from around the Pacific Northwest. Open most afternoons. Admission is by donation.

Myrtlewood. You've seen the signs and shops lining the highway up and down the coast, and by now you're either thinking, "Oy, what's with this myrtlewood already?" or else you can't wait to get your hands on that special five-piece nut dish set carved out of the golden wood. Myrtlewood is big business in these parts. If you insist on stopping, pull over at the House of Myrtlewood (1125 S First Street; (503) 267-7804 or (800) 255-5318) for a free 20-minute tour of the myrtlewood factory, and see wood-turners, carvers, and finishers in action.

Restaurants

BLUE HERON BISTRO

Voilà, a real bistro with European flair in the heart of Coos Bay. Airy atmosphere, indoor and outdoor tables (overlooking the sidewalk traffic), and an innovative menu, priced reasonably. Owner Wim de Vriend keeps people coming back at all times of day: for waffles, breakfast parfaits (yogurt, fruit, and muesli), and good strong jolts of joe in the morning. For an array of salads and sandwiches (such as blackened snapper on a toasted onion roll with green chiles) or a German sausage plate at lunch. For handcrafted pasta or continent-hopping cuisine at dinner. This is where you'll find the coast's finest apple pie. *Hwy 101 and Commercial; (503) 267-3933; 100 W Commercial, Coos Bay; $$; beer and wine; MC, V; local checks only; breakfast, lunch, dinner every day.*

KUM-YON'S

Kum-Yon has transformed a nondescript eatery into a showcase of South Korean cuisine. Some Japanese (sushi, sashimi) and Chinese (egg-flower soup, fried rice, chow mein) dishes are offered, but to discover

what really makes this place special,
you'll have to venture into the un-
known. Try spicy hot *chap-chae* (trans-
parent noodles pan-fried with veggies
and beef) or *bulgoki* (thinly sliced sir-
loin marinated in honey and spices).
Get there early on weekends. *On the
south end of the main drag; (503) 269-
2662; 835 S Broadway, Coos Bay; $; beer
and wine; MC, V; local checks only;
lunch, dinner every day.*

Lodgings

COOS BAY MANOR BED AND BREAKFAST INN

☆

Head up the hill away from the commercial glitz of Highway 101 and you'll
discover beautifully restored homes
among deciduous and coniferous
trees and flowering shrubs. The Coos
Bay Manor is such a place, on a quiet
residential street with a panoramic
waterfront view. The view is even more
stunning from the upstairs balcony
patio where Patricia Williams serves
breakfast on mellow summer morn-
ings. The guest rooms are all distinc-
tively decorated (the cattle baron's
room is decked out with bear and
coyote rugs) and sport comfortable
feather beds. Mannerly children and

dogs (which tolerate cats) are welcome. *On S 5th, 4 blocks above the waterfront; (503) 269-1224 or (800) 269-1224; 955 S 5th St, Coos Bay, OR 97420; $$; no credit cards; checks OK.*

BLACKBERRY INN   ¢

Guests here have the renovated 1903 Victorian home to themselves, as the owners live elsewhere. Breakfast is a continental affair, but a kitchen is available, with eggs and bread supplied. A night in the small but adequate Rose Room is a genuine bargain, especially in urbanized Coos Bay. Unfortunately, the inn is located on a busy thoroughfare. *Next to Taco Bell, downtown; (503) 267-6951; 843 Central Ave, Coos Bay, OR 97420; $; MC, V; checks OK.*

Charleston

For an exhilarating side trip and gorgeous sunsets, get off Highway 101 and head west about 10 miles on the Cape Arago Highway to Charleston and beyond, back to the wildly beautiful shore. Charleston is the third-largest commercial port on the coast, as the piscatorial scent in the air reveals; industry here includes fish-processing plants for tuna, salmon, oysters, and

"I don't like oysters, but I've got one guy out here, if he gets hungry out in the field, he'll stop, pick one up, shuck it, and pop it in his mouth. I've seen oysters here that are 8 to 12 inches across — big as a guy's forearm. I found an oyster that has the start of seven little pearls all in a 9-inch shell."

— Stacy Heathcock, manager of an oyster harvesting crew

shrimp. Not surprisingly, it's a great place to find some of the tastiest seafood dishes anywhere on the coast, or pick up fresh picnic and barbecue fixings on your way to the nearby state parks.

 Qualman Oyster Farms (4898 Crown Point Road; (503) 888-3145), in business since 1937, is the largest producer of oysters on the south Oregon coast. With 235 acres of oyster beds, it produces up to 6,000 gallons of bluepoint oysters per year. These "stick-grown" oysters are more easily harvested than traditionally raised oysters and are quickly transferred for shucking. Stick-growing produces larger (as big as your hand), cleaner shellfish (about $4 a dozen). Qualman Farms is just a few miles south of Coos Bay; follow signs from Cape Arago Highway. Open Monday–Saturday.

 Sunset Bay State Park (Cape Arago Highway; (503) 888-4902) has a pretty, vest-pocket cove hemmed in by 50-foot cliffs — a good spot to dip your feet or take a swim, especially for kids. With a palisade of rocks guarding its seaward side, the cove is perpetually calm, even during midwinter sou'westers, when a colossal surf rages a couple of hundred yards

Cape Arago State Park overlooks the Oregon Islands National Wildlife Refuge, home to birds, seals, and sea lions. The Oregon Coast Trail winds along the clifftops here, and connects with the Shore Acres and Sunset Bay.

offshore. Day use is free. There is a grassy picnic and year-round camping area nearby, as well as public golf course.

> **Lumber Baron's Estate.** Shore Acres State Park (13030 Cape Arago Highway, Charleston, OR 97420; (503) 888-3732) is a thousand-acre coastal gem and the former estate of lumber and shipping baron Louis J. Simpson. His original summer home grew over the years into a mansion with an indoor pool and elaborately landscaped grounds. The home burned down in 1921 and was replaced, but by the 1940s all the property had been donated or sold to the state of Oregon. Unable to maintain Simpson's former home, the state razed it in 1948.

What remains are the gardener's cottage (the second mansion's former dining-room wing), formal gardens, and breathtaking cliff-edge views. The beautifully maintained botanical gardens include a Japanese lily pond, rose gardens, a greenhouse, and exotic plantings from around the world. Several trails run through the forested property, leading along the clifftops and down to a secluded little cove.

From the viewing gazebo perched atop a dramatic bluff, you can watch the storms piling up offshore. On either side, the layered sedimentary rocks have been carved into almost organic patterns and formations. Tilted upward, they face the furious swells like a ship's prow, sending white fountains of spray some 80 feet into the air. Admission to the park is free. It's open during daylight hours year-round.

⊠ Estuary Reserve. South Slough National Estuarine Research Reserve (PO Box 5417, Charleston, OR 97420; (503) 888-5558) protects 4,500 acres of tidal habitat, salt marshes, mudflats, and woodlands set aside for research, education, and recreation. Hiking, bird-watching, and canoeing are the most popular activities. At the reserve interpretive center, get maps, directions, and personal guides. Open every day in summer, weekdays only from Labor Day to Memorial Day.

The Estuary Study Trail is a 3-mile round trip, beginning at the center. Descending 300 feet on a graded hill, it follows Hidden Creek down to the slough, where habitats change from forest to swamp and marsh. At the bottom of the marsh, a lookout is set up for viewing indigenous birdlife. Allow two hours for the hike.

The Wasson Creek Trail, down Seven Devils Road from the estuary reserve, is just three-quarters of a mile, with moderate-to-easy walking through meadow and forest. Songbirds, birds of prey, elk, beaver, and deer frequent the area. Allow 45 minutes.

 The harborside Oregon Institute of Marine Biology, headquartered here, is not open to visitors, but in summer it does set up a public display near the boat basin, with interpretive exhibits and tanks filled with various live sea creatures. Late June–September. Call for more information, (503) 888-2581.

  Since 1979, Oregon Coast Music Festival (Box 663, Coos Bay, OR 97420; (503) 267-0938) has gathered an impressively heady roster of American and international performers for concerts in Reedsport, Coos Bay/ North Bend, and Bandon. The eclectic series, held over the second half of July, includes just about everything from baroque to folk, spiced with jazz, Broadway show tunes, and chamber and orchestral works. Past highlights have included brass ensemble concerts *en plein air* in the lovely gardens at Shore Acres State Park, and organ recitals on the vintage Wurlitzer in Coos Bay's classic Egyptian Theatre. Series passes are available; some events are free.

Restaurants

PORTSIDE

It's dark and cavernous inside, so you'll notice the lighted glass tanks

containing live crabs and lobsters –
a good sign that the kitchen is con-
cerned with fresh ingredients. From
your table you can watch fishing gear
being repaired and vessels coming
and going, since you're right at the
Charleston Boat Basin. Naturally,
fresh seafood, simply prepared, is
the house specialty. Fridays there's
a sumptuous Chinese seafood buffet
that includes everything but the an-
chor. *Just over the Charleston bridge, in
the midst of the boat basin; (503) 888-
5544; 8001 Kingfisher Rd, Charleston;
$$; full bar; AE, DC, MC, V; local checks
only; lunch, dinner every day.*

Bandon

A self-proclaimed storm-watching
hot spot and cranberry capital,
Bandon looks – and feels – newly
painted, freshly scrubbed, and friendly.
Some locals believe that Bandon rests
on a "ley line," an underground crys-
talline structure reputed to be the
focus of powerful cosmic energies.
Maybe so. What's certain is that,
with one of the most developed and
thriving of the coast's "old towns,"
Bandon's magnetism does seem to
lure visitors right off the adjacent
highway to stroll around the shops,

Cape Blanco State Park has camping and day-use facilities near the lighthouse, amid Sitka spruce forests and berry bushes. Nearby lie the eerie remnants of a cemetery and church, Mary, Star of the Sea, built by Patrick Hughes and once used by area settlers.

galleries, and cafes of its compact center.

Capes and Lighthouses. Wind-hammered Cape Blanco, with its 1870 lighthouse, is the most westerly point in the Lower 48. Furious Pacific Ocean storms, making their first landfall here, seem to take this fact personally, and they pummel Cape Blanco with all their might: winds here have been clocked at over 180 miles per hour.

Cape Blanco State Park, (503) 332-6774, carved out of the 1,800-acre Hughes dairy ranch, covers most of the cape. The historic Hughes House, down in the lowlands beside the Sixes River, was built in 1898 for $3,800 by R. J. Lindberg for the Hughes family. The two-story, 11-room cedar house, listed on the National Register of Historic Places as a prime example of Eastlake Victorian architecture, is a curious anomaly out here on this isolated, rugged coast.

Cranberries. The naturally acidic, peaty soil of this area has proved ideal for raising cranberries, and Bandon has almost 1,000 acres under cultivation. The September Cranberry Festival, a 50-year tradition, pays tribute to the town's foremost fruit. Four days of community celebration include an

The cranberry jam at the family-run Misty Meadows roadside stand (Highway 101 south of Bandon; (503) 347-2575) is a perennial favorite. The family has been producing coveted jellies, jams, and syrups for a quarter of a century, and is reportedly the oldest cottage industry in the state.

arts-and-crafts show, float parades through Old Town, kite-flying contests, the crowning of the Cranberry Queen, tours of the cranberry bogs, and a food fair in which competitors vie to create the most imaginative cranberry dishes. Good old-fashioned fun.

 For local treats, stop in at locally renowned Cranberry Sweets (501 First Street; (503) 347-9475), where they concoct such delectables as cranberry truffles, cranberry candy, fudge, and other treats. They ship all over, and their confections have even caught the attention of the *New York Times*. The staff is friendly, and very generous with samples. Open daily.

 One of the southern coast's best bookstores is Winter River Books and Gallery (170 Second Street; (503) 347-4111). It's a light, inviting place, with a balanced selection of literature, travel, new age, health, art books, and magazines.

 Though less well known than its larger counterpart in Tillamook, Bandon's Cheddar Cheese Factory (Highway 101, just north of Bandon; (800) 548-8961) is worth a stop to see cheese being made by hand as it has been for over a century at one of the last of the many cheese plants that once thrived along the coast. The Bandon plant's history began during the 1880s, when fresh milk was transported by sternwheeler. The "full cream cheddar," made from whole Jersey milk, soon became sought after for its rich flavor. Today, they still age some varieties of cheese up to 24 months. In addition to several cheddars, they also produce Monterey Jack, Colby, and flavored cheeses; samples available.

 Budget gourmets will appreciate the inexpensive "walk-away" seafood cocktails at the Bandon Fisheries Market (First and Chicago; (503) 347-2851). They make for a quick, tasty meal to munch at harborside tables. Other delicacies here include smoked trout and salmon, shrimp, and crab.

 Horseback ride on the beach? Rent a horse by the hour at Bandon Beach Riding Stables (2640 Beach Loop Drive; (503) 347-3423), which has 30 horses to ride and always a lot of colts to watch frolic (11 born in 1994). They take people (all ages) out to the beach to ride, do buggy rides at Christmastime, and parade their draft horses in the off-season.

Boice-Cope County Park is the site of the large freshwater Floras Lake, popular with boaters, anglers, and board sailors. An extensive trail network invites hiking and mountain biking (take the hike to isolated Blacklock Point).

 A good place for exploring is Bullards Beach State Park, on Highway 101 1 mile north of Bandon. It occupies an expansive 1,266 acres crosscut with hiking and biking trails that lead to uncrowded driftwood- and kelp-cluttered beaches. The 1896 Coquille River Lighthouse is a beauty, located across the dunes at the end of the park's main road. The tower is not open to the public, but the attached main building, with informational plaques and great views of the Coquille River mouth, is.

 South of Bandon, the landscape opens to reveal sparsely forested ocher hills dotted with thousands of grazing sheep. Heading out of town, a scenic alternative to the highway is Beach Loop Road (good for cycling). It parallels the ocean in view of a welter of sea-sculpted offshore rock formations, with evocative names such as Devil's Kitchen and Elephant Rock. The best known, Face Rock, is said to portray an Indian princess turned to stone by an evil spirit.

 Sand Sculpture. Bandon's annual Sandcastle/Sandsculpture Contest (Ray Kelley, PO Box 335, Bandon, OR 97411; (503) 347-2511), held on Memorial Day, is always a big hit. Individuals

Big grassy areas for kite flying and year-round camping (192 sites total) and horse-camping facilities can be found at Bullards Beach State Park, 1 mile north of Bandon; (503) 347-2209. Good wind-surfing beaches abound on the river and ocean sides of the park.

and teams, from preschool age and up, compete for prizes and if not their 15 minutes of fame, then at least the sort that lasts till high tide comes in. Starts in early morning, on the beach at Seabird Lane and Beach Loop Road.

▶ Coquille Point Wildlife Park was recently designated a wildlife park to protect the nesting seabird colonies on the adjacent rocks, part of the Oregon Islands National Wildlife Refuge. Six acres of weather-beaten coastal headland have been reshaped, layered with topsoil, and planted with native vegetation.

Still under development at press time, park plans call for a wheelchair-accessible pedestrian trail to take visitors through the area. Interpretive postings will include information on nesting seabirds (murres, guillemots, tufted puffins, and others), marine mammals, bird migration, and the Coquille Estuary. For information, contact Shoreline Education for Awareness (SEA) (PO Box 957, Bandon, OR 97411; (503) 347-3683). SEA members can be found in the point parking lot every Saturday morning from mid-spring to late summer.

▶ Lions, Tigers, and Bears (Oh, My!)
You don't expect to find snow leop-

ards and Siberian lynx on the southern Oregon coast, but the West Coast Game Park (Route 1, Box 1330, Bandon, OR 97411; (503) 347-3106), 7 miles south of Bandon on Highway 101, is home to these big cats and another 75 domestic and exotic animal species. At the country's largest wild animal petting park, you'll also see lions, tigers, bears, cougars, antelope, peacocks, monkeys, camels, bison, zebras – some 450 birds and animals in all – on 26 wooded acres.

Be prepared for a closer encounter than you'll get at most zoos. Adult animals pace back and forth in large viewing pens (scrutinizing you just as much as you do them), but their offspring are available for petting. To accustom them to human contact, public relations director Debbie Tramell says, animals are hand-raised by park employees. "They even take the animals home with them at night for feeding purposes. Lion cubs need to be bottle-fed every two hours," Tramell says. Once the young animals mature beyond petting age, some are moved to zoos; others are trained for stage and screen. Open daily March–November, weather permitting. Winter hours vary.

Restaurants

SEA STAR BISTRO

If Bandon encapsulates the coast –
dramatic seascapes, quaint atmosphere, unspoiled beaches, good eats
and sleeps, even a lighthouse and a
free daily morning news sheet – the
Sea Star encapsulates Bandon. The
Sea Star began years ago as a friendly
hostel. In time, it grew to include
more private accommodations and a
small bistro. Today, the guest house is
also home to one of Bandon's better
restaurants. The bistro serves healthy,
somewhat low-fat but quite craveable
international dishes. New owners
Eileen Sexton and Bob O'Neal en-
deavor to use locally grown, fresh
ingredients, and keep the chalkboard
menu flexible. The place is small (no
smoking) and there's a newspaper,
magazine, and travel book reading
table to help pass the time – located
in the alcove that connects to the
hostel.

The guest house ($35–$70), with
natural wood interior, skylights, and
harbor-view deck, offers a comparatively lavish alternative to the hostel
next door. The less formal neighbor
(connected to the guest house by a

courtyard) offers small men's and women's dorms, private rooms for couples and families, a common room, kitchen, secluded courtyard, and sun decks. *Take 2nd St off Hwy 101 into Old Town; (503) 347-9632; 375 2nd St, Bandon; $$; beer and wine; MC, V; local checks only; breakfast, lunch every day, dinner Wed-Sun.*

Andrea's

Andrea Gatov's eclectic south coast restaurant continues to be very popular, in part because it doubles as the unofficial information hub of Bandon. Breakfasts are filling. Substantial sandwiches on homemade whole-grain breads and soups are on the lunch menu. For dinner, Gatov draws on many traditions, from Cajun to Russian. She's strong on seafood too. Her lamb is home-raised. And on Friday nights, locals descend on the place for pizza. Sunday brunch might include seafood hash or apple cranberry blintzes, always accompanied by Bandon's best cup of coffee. *1 block east of ocean; (503) 347-3022; 160 Baltimore, Bandon; $$; beer and wine; no credit cards; checks OK; breakfast, lunch Mon-Sat, dinner every day (Fri-Sat only during winter), brunch Sun.*

BANDON BOATWORKS ☆

A local favorite, the Boatworks takes advantage of its two-story location near the south jetty on the Coquille River to provide fine dining with an equally fine view. If the restaurant is packed, wait for a table upstairs; it's a shame to miss the sunset on the river and ocean. Dinner selections might include baked butterflied shrimp served in a light and tangy mustard sauce, and fresh oysters roasted in anisette. The salad bar includes warm loaves of sweet, crumbly cranberry bread (local berries, of course). *Follow River Rd out to the jetty; (503) 347-2111; S Jetty Rd, Bandon; $$; beer and wine; AE, DC, DIS, MC, V; checks OK; lunch, dinner Tues-Sun (closed Jan).*

HARP'S ☆

Don't look for unusual background music. The name is derived from the presence of owner/chef Michael Harpster. Do look for some wonderful halibut. The house pasta comes with scampi and a sauce of hot pepper and lemon. And the filet mignon is marinated in garlic and teriyaki. Harpster does a good job with his house sweet onion soup made with beef broth and cognac. If your chair leans sideways a bit, blame the old floors in the build-

Sleep aboard an authentic sternwheeler reproduction. The **Na-So-Mah** is the inspiration and creation of former home builder Joe Bolduc, who operates this floating inn year-round with his wife, Dixie. The Riverboat B&B (moored on the Coquille River, (503) 347-1922) remains moored at night and, weather permitting, casts off at 7:30am on a 2¹/₂-hour cruise up the Coquille River during breakfast.

ing. ¹/₂ *block east of ocean; (503) 347-9057; 130 Chicago St, Bandon; $$; beer and wine; AE, MC, V; checks OK; dinner every day (Tues-Sat in winter).*

Lodgings

LIGHTHOUSE BED AND BREAKFAST

Spacious and appealing, this contemporary has windows opening toward the Coquille River, its lighthouse, and the ocean. Nonsmoking guests can watch fishing boats, seals, and seabirds nearby or stroll into Old Town. Two rooms view the ocean; the others look at the river and the town. The Green House Room – with king bed, fireplace, whirlpool tub, and TV – is the true stunner. *1st St at 650 Jetty Rd; (503) 347-9316; PO Box 24, Bandon, OR 97411; $$; MC, V; checks OK.*

INN AT FACE ROCK

This elegant resort is just across the road from the beach. Choose from one-bedroom to two-bedroom two-bath suites with kitchens, fireplaces, and balconies. Many rooms have views, and prices vary as dramatically as the weather. The Jacuzzi is exclusive to guests; the nine-hole golf course, restaurant, and bar are not.

The resort's golf pros can give you a lesson in coping with the often irritating winds. You can find better dining elsewhere. *2 miles south of Bandon, right turn at Seabird Lane; (503) 347-9441 or (800) 638-3092; 3225 Beach Loop Rd, Bandon, OR 97411; $$; AE, DC, DIS, MC, V; checks OK..*

WINDERMERE MOTEL ☆

Many guests wouldn't change a thing about this quintessential family motel. Where else can you find wonderfully battered oceanside cottages with kitchenettes and room for kids to run, all at moderate rates? Rooms are clustered in units of three or four; the best are those with sleeping lofts, but all have truly magnificent ocean views and access to an uncrowded beach. No pets, and they mean it. *1 1/2 miles south of Bandon, west on Seabird Lane; (503) 347-3710; 3250 Beach Loop Rd, Bandon, OR 97411; $$; AE, MC, V; no checks.*

BANDON WAYSIDE MOTEL ¢

This 10-unit, out-of-the-way motel occupies a parklike setting on the road to Coquille. Rooms (less than $35) are simple and clean, with an outdoor barbecue in the large backyard. This quiet isolation, 2 miles from the beach, occasionally spares the visitor from the summer coastal fog. House-broken pets are allowed at no extra charge in some units. *1 block off Hwy 101 at 42 S; (503) 347-3421; Hwy 42 S, Bandon, OR 97411; $; MC, V; no checks.*

SUNSET MOTEL   ¢

Everywhere along the coast, the closer you get to the ocean, the more expensive the room. The Sunset, just across Beach Loop Road from the ocean, is a worthwhile compromise. A clean, comfortable room with a limited view and a double bed is yours for $50, while an oceanfront unit is more than twice as much. All rooms include TV, use of an indoor Jacuzzi, and morning coffee. *1755 Beach Loop Road; (503) 347-2453 or (800) 842-2407; PO Box 373, Bandon, OR 97411; $; AE, DIS, MC, V; checks OK.*

Port Orford

Port Orford, the most westerly incorporated city in the continental United States, is also the rainiest place on the Oregon Coast. That doesn't bother most locals, who will tell you that what matters are its relaxed pace and terrific views.

Oregon's oldest coastal town, Port Orford is far removed from big-city

Don't miss the ocean-side drive. Follow the Ocean View signs (painted with a huge arrow on the pavement). Once over the little hill, you get a panoramic view of the harbor, Humbug Mountain, and Battle Rock — an offshore promontory where in 1851 local Indians fought white settlers in one of the state's fiercest conflicts ever between Natives and whites.

nuances, yet hip in its own way, especially considering the seasonal influx of board sailors and surfers, who head for Battle Rock and Hubbard's Creek beaches.

 After commercial fishers and lumbermen, painters, weavers, sculptors, quilt makers, glassblowers, and other artisans make up a good portion of Port Orford's population of 1,100 or so. During the first week of May, the three-day Port Orford Arts Festival celebrates the visual and performing arts throughout the community. Galleries open their doors to all, the town hosts visual displays and performances, and craftspersons demonstrate their talents, all complemented by gourmet food booths. (Call (503) 332-0045 for details.)

 Towering darkly over the coast, mist-shrouded Humbug Mountain State Park rises 1,750 feet above sea level. State park campsites (April–October) are located at the base of the massive headland, 6 miles south of Port Orford.

 A day-use area for Humbug Mountain State Park is three-quarters of a mile southeast of the campground entrance bordering Brush Creek. A scenic 3-mile path curves out of Brush

Port Orford, on a bulge of land jutting prominently into deep water, is a premier whale-watching location. Occasionally, single whales and small pods of gray whales spend all year in the quiet, kelp-protected coves found here.

Creek Canyon all the way up to the windblown peak. The Oregon Coast Trail also threads through Humbug Mountain State Park north from Rocky Point, passing the campground and emerging before the registration booth.

On the way to the top, trailblazers will encounter gigantic rhododendrons in bloom and eye-popping views of black-sand beaches and rocky, kelp-strewn shorelines. For complete trail information, contact Humbug Mountain State Park, (503) 332-6774.

▶ **Dinosaurs.** There's no way you can miss the 25-foot-tall *Tyrannosaurus rex* standing out front, so you may as well pull over and have a closer look. No, it's not a leftover movie set from *The Flintstones,* but it does qualify as one of the Oregon coast's certifiably wackier – albeit educational – attractions.

The Prehistoric Gardens (36848 Highway 101 S, Port Orford, OR 97465; (503) 332-4463) are the brainchild of sculptor and self-taught paleontologist E. V. Nelson, who started creating life-size dinosaurs in 1953. Now, in addition to *T. rex*, there are another 22 mammoth models – including triceratops, pterodactyl, and stegosaurus –

Fisherpersons should visit the Elk and Sixes Rivers for their dynamite salmon and steelhead runs.

fashioned from steel and concrete and painted in unexpectedly bright hues. They're placed around the appropriately primeval setting of fern-choked rain forest, identified and explained by informative plaques. Younger kids especially will enjoy this. Admission: adults $5.50; children 12–18 $4.50, 5–11 $3.50. Open year-round every day. Yearly rainfall here can reach 10 feet, so complimentary umbrellas are provided.

Restaurants

CB's BISTRO (SIXES RIVER HOTEL)

This turn-of-the-century farmhouse, once part of a sheep ranch, is now a French restaurant with four guest rooms (rates include breakfast). Chef/owner Christophe Baudry prepares a fine tortellini and prawns dish, as well as roasted rabbit, Thai chicken, jambalaya, and lamb chops. Presentation, with elegant vegetables and fresh herbs, is superior. The wine list, posted on a blackboard, is heavily French and a bit spendy. The intimate dining room seats only about a dozen people, so reservations are a must. *Turn east off Hwy 101 onto Sixes River Rd at town of Sixes, watch for driveway*

¼ mile on right; (503) 332-3900 or
(800) 828-5161; P.O. Box 327, Sixes;
$$; full bar; MC, V; dinner Tues-Sun.

TRUCULENT OYSTER RESTAURANT AND PEG LEG SALOON

Enter the dark nautical interior of the Truculent Oyster through the Peg Leg Saloon. The fresh oyster shooters, homemade soups (clam chowder, split pea with ham), weekend prime rib, and mild Mexican entrées are the strong points of an eclectic menu. The slow-broiled chinook salmon (seasonal) can be outstanding. Portions are sizable, service prompt, and coffee miserable. *At the south end of town; (503) 332-9461; 236 6th St, Port Orford; $$; full bar; AE, MC, V; local checks only; lunch Thurs-Sun, dinner every day.*

Lodgings

FLORAS LAKE HOUSE BED AND BREAKFAST

If the hot summer sun beckons you to cool swims in a freshwater lake, choose Floras. This modern two-story house offers four spacious rooms, each with private bath and access to a deck, two with fireplaces. The two most elegant are the North Room with its garden decor and the South Room with four-poster king bed; however, you can see Floras Lake and the ocean beyond from all rooms. Hiking and biking trails abound, and you might just have the beach at Floras Lake all to yourself. *From Hwy 101, turn W on Floras Lake Rd, 9 mi N of Port Orford, and follow signs to Boice Cope Park; (503) 348-2573; 92870 Boice Cope Rd, Langlois, OR 97450; $$$; DIS, MC, V; checks OK.*

HOME BY THE SEA BED AND BREAKFAST ☆

The ocean view is one of southern Oregon's best, and you can see it from both guest rooms in this modest, homey B&B that sits atop a bluff near Battle Rock. Guests have the run of a large dining/living room area, also with ocean view. Quiche, waffles, omelets, and fresh strawberries are the Mitchells' morning mainstays. *1 block west of Hwy 101 at 444 Jackson St; (503) 332-2855; PO Box 606-B, Port Orford, OR 97465-06069; $$; MC, V; checks OK.*

CASTAWAY BY THE SEA

This bluff-top 14-unit, two-story motel sits on history: ancient Indian artifacts, plus the former sites of both

Fort Orford, the oldest military installation on the Oregon coast, and the Castaway Lodge, once frequented by Jack London. The two three-bedroom units have kitchenettes and glassed-in sun decks with harbor and ocean views. Avoid the dank older section under the office, except in a pinch. It's an easy stroll to the beach, harbor, or shops. *Between Ocean and Harbor on W 5th; (503) 332-4502; PO Box 844, Port Orford, OR 97465; $$; MC, V; local checks only.*

BATTLE ROCK MOTEL   ¢

Although this nothin'-fancy, retro-looking motel is on the wrong side of Highway 101, your room ($40 for two) is only a stone's throw from the cliffside trail of Battle Rock Wayside Park (a good whale-watching vista) and a wonderful stretch of uncrowded beach. You're also within walking distance of most of the rest of Port Orford. *Off Hwy 101 at 136 S 6th; (503) 332-7331; PO Box 288, Port Orford, OR 97465; $; MC, V; no checks.*

Gold Beach

Named by 1850s miners for its once gold-laced sands, Gold Beach squeezes in snugly between the

For deep-sea fishing, check with Briggs Charters at the Port of Gold Beach, (503) 247-7150, providing bait and tackle for four-hour excursions (July–September).

"Tourists call me in February to book a trip on August 22, then ask me what the weather's going to be like on that day."
– Receptionist for Rogue River Outfitters

coastal headlands and the Pacific. The Rogue River – one of the dozen U.S. Wild and Scenic Rivers, renowned for its fabulous salmon and steelhead runs – divides Gold Beach from neighboring Wedderburn. Outdoorsman-author Zane Grey is numbered among the river's many admirers, and his writings helped bring the area to the world's attention.

 Angling Dreams. Gold Beach is an angler's heaven: salmon, steelhead, cutthroat trout, and giant sturgeon swim the Rogue; snapper, cod, coho salmon, and perch are found offshore. For information on individual licensed guides, stop by or call the Chamber of Commerce for an extensive list; or contact the Rogue Outdoor Store (560 N Ellensburg Avenue, Gold Beach, OR 97444; (503) 247-7142), where you can also get fishing tips and rent tackle or clam shovels.

 River Trips on the Rogue. Just north of Gold Beach, Wedderburn is the home port of the Rogue River Mailboat, which has been mail carrier to folks upriver in Agness since 1895, when it was a two-day haul. Out of that necessary service has grown a busy recreational industry for several local operators, who whisk passengers

Rogue River Outfitters, (503) 247-2684, offers white-water raft tours as well as fishing trips. The drift-fishing trip for fall steelhead includes equipment, lodging, food, and guide fees for $750 per person. A day-long fishing trip on the Rogue can be arranged any time of the year on the outfitter's covered boat. Fall steelhead are fished September–November. The bigger winter steelhead are fished January–early March.

on jet boat tours far into the scenic interior in just a couple of hours. River Rogue Mailboat Trips offers three different trips up the river to view harbor seals, ospreys, bald eagles, blue herons, black bear, blacktail deer, and other wildlife. The "Postage Due" trip is 64 miles long and takes you up to Agness. This is the gentlest ride and includes a two-hour meal break in Agness. The "Special Delivery" trip is 80 miles of white water through backcountry and includes a two-hour meal break in Agness. The "Handle With Care" is a 104-mile jet trip "up the down staircase." Not for the faint of heart: you'll ride a 1,000-plus-horsepower hydro-jet as far up river as the boat can go. For reservations or more information, call (800) 458-3511, or stop by for same-day reservations at their dock on Rogue River Road; heading south, take the left before crossing the Patterson Bridge over the Rogue River.

Another jet boat company offering three similar tours from the port of Gold Beach is Jerry's Rogue Jets; call (503) 247-7601 for more information.

 White-water raft traffic on the all-too-popular Wild and Scenic part of the Rogue is carefully controlled. River runners interested in unsupervised trips must sign up with the U.S. Forest Service, (503) 479-3735, for a lottery during the first six weeks in the new year.

>> Trails cut deep into the Kalmiopsis Wilderness and Siskiyou National Forest, or you can follow the Rogue River. A jet boat will drop you off to explore all or part of the 40-mile-long Rogue River Trail along the north bank. Spring is the best time for a trek, before 90-degree heat makes the rock-face trail intolerable. Stay at any of seven remote lodges, where — for prices ranging from $55 to $180 per night — you end your day with a hot shower and dinner, and begin the next with breakfast and sack lunch. (Reservations are a must.) Rogue River Reservations dispenses information and can arrange booking on just about any Rogue River outing, jet boat trip, or overnight stay in the wilderness; (503) 247-6504 or (800) 525-2161.

>> The Pistol River area (8 miles south of Gold Beach, Nesika Beach (7 miles north), and Rocky Point (25 miles north) beckon tide poolers with miniature sea life spread among the rocks and sand. Sea anemones, mollusks, urchins, starfish, and tiny

Rock Hunting. These days you'll find more agate and jasper than gold along the beaches outside of Gold Beach. Large trees and logs drift ashore, and storms deposit surf-washed agates, jasper, and the occasional fossil or Japanese glass float. The best beach-combing happens during the winter months, after a heavy storm. Go searching for agates and other semiprecious stones at low and high tides, when the waves churn the beach gravel, revealing nature's bounty.

hermit crabs dwell within each perfect ecosystem.

 ❯ The Whale of a Wine Festival, in mid-January, takes place at the Curry County Fairgrounds Saturday noon–7pm, Sun. noon–5pm. A $6 admission ticket buys you a souvenir wine glass and a chance to win door prizes. Inside, sample Oregon's finest wines, dine at local restaurant food booths, watch seminars on whale migration, check out the arts and crafts, and sample gourmet coffees.

 ❯ Cape Sebastian State Park lies at the end of a steep road, accessed via Highway 101 7 miles south of Gold Beach. The real spectacle begins at the south parking lot. Atop the headland rising 700 feet above the sea, you'll be able to see 40–50 miles north or south on a clear day. A 2-mile trail snakes from the south parking lot through dense greenery down to the surf, where you're likely to have miles of empty beach to yourself. Open from sunup to sundown.

Restaurants

THE CAPTAIN'S TABLE

This is Gold Beach's old favorite, though the seafood can be inconsis-

The Rogue River Jet Boat Marathon in mid-June kicks off with "Calcutta" on Friday night, the big to-do before the race — everyone's welcome. On Saturday, the racers take off from Jot's Resort (on the estuary, north side of the bridge; (800) 367-5687) and go up to Agness; spectators gather at Jot's for the grand finale.

tently prepared. The corn-fed beef from Kansas City is meat you can't often get this far west. One nice touch: help yourself to as much salad as you want. The dining area is moderately small, furnished with antiques, and can get smoky from the popular bar. Both dining room and bar have nice ocean views. The staff is courteous, enthusiastic, and speedy. *Hwy 101, south end of town; (503) 247-6308; 1295 S Ellensburg Ave, Gold Beach; $$; full bar; MC, V; local checks only; dinner every day.*

NOR'WESTER ☆

From the windows of the Nor'Wester, you may watch fishermen delivering your meal: local sole, snapper, halibut, lingcod, and salmon. Most seafood is served simply: broiled or sautéed, perhaps sprinkled with some almonds. You can also find a decent steak, or chicken with Dijon glaze. Dinners feature both soup and salad, served simultaneously. *On the waterfront; (503) 247-2333; Port of Gold Beach, Gold Beach; $$; full bar; AE, MC, V; checks OK; dinner every day.*

Lodgings

TU TU'TUN LODGE

★★★

The lodge is one of the loveliest on the coast, even though you are 7 miles inland. Tall, mist-cloudy trees line the north shore of the Rogue River. The building is handsomely designed, with such niceties as private porches overlooking the river, racks to hold fishing gear, and stylish, rustic decor throughout. There are 16 units in the two-story main building and 2 larger, noisier kitchen suites in the lodge. In the apple orchard is a lovely garden house (sleeps six) with old stone fireplace. You can swim in the heated lap pool, use the four-hole pitch-and-putt course, play horseshoes, relax around the mammoth rock fireplace, hike, or fish.

Three family-style meals a day are served. The prix-fixe dinner begins with hors d'oeuvres in the bar. Your own fish might be the entrée, or perhaps chicken breasts with a champagne sauce, or prime rib. Only the two river suites and garden house are available in winter (restaurant open May–October only). *Follow the Rogue River from the bridge up the north bank for 7 miles; (503) 247-6664; 96550*

*North Bank Rogue, Gold Beach, OR
97444; $$$; full bar; MC, V; checks OK.*

INN AT NESIKA BEACH

This three-story Victorian-style home
built in 1992 is spacious and grand,
and on the ocean, too. It has quickly
caught on with southern Oregonians
as a romantic destination. Guests
have the run of both a living room and
parlor, where wine is offered each
evening. Breakfast, served in the for-
mal dining room, may include crêpes,
scones, fresh asparagus, and home-
made muffins. Most of the oversize
bedrooms enjoy ocean views, fire-
places, and two-person Jacuzzis. *West
off Hwy 101 on Nesika Rd 5 miles north
of Gold Beach; (503) 247-6434; 33026
Nesika Rd, Gold Beach, OR 97444; $$;
no credit cards; checks OK.*

GOLD BEACH RESORT

If you want a fairly fancy motel room
with a good ocean view, this is probably your best bet in Gold Beach. It's
just an easy walk to the beach. During
the summer season the 39 units range
from $79 for a standard room to $125
and up for a condo with fireplace and
kitchen. There's an indoor swimming
pool and Jacuzzi. *Hwy 101, near south
end of town, (503) 247-7066 or (800)*

541-0947; 1330 S Ellensburg Ave, Gold
Beach, OR 97444; $$; AE, DC, DIS,
MC, V; no checks.

JOT'S RESORT ☆

The manicured grounds of this lovely
resort spread out on the north bank of
the Rogue River near the historic
Rogue River Bridge; the lights (and the
traffic) of Gold Beach are just across
the river. The 140 rooms are spacious
and tastefully decorated, and many
have refrigerators. There's an indoor
pool, spa, and weight room. Rent a
bike (or a boat!) to explore the river-
front. Rogue River jet boats and
guided fishing trips leave right from
the resort's docks. An unexpected
fishing trip? The lodge rents necessary
gear. *At the Rogue River Bridge, at
94630 Wedderburn Loop; (503) 247-
6676 or (800) 367-5687; PO Box J, Gold
Beach, OR 97444; $$; AE, DC, DIS,
MC, V; checks OK.*

Brookings

Just 6 miles north of the border, in the
heart of what's known as the Banana
Belt for its mild year-round climate,
Brookings is a booming retirement
community for Oregonians and Cali-
fornians. But more than retirees thrive

Brookings is promoting eco-tourism these days in order to keep its visiting whales and geese, frolicking elk, black bear, sea lions, and steadfast redwoods from disappearing. If you have a penchant for preservation, the Chamber of Commerce would be happy to accommodate you: choose from tide pool cleanup, erosion control, and habitat improvement; (800) 535-9468.

in the warm winter and early spring; lilies (90 percent of the U.S. supply) and azaleas grow en masse in maintained gardens.

With one of the safest harbors on all the Oregon Coast, Brookings is also a busy port town. The contemporary sprawl has obscured some of Brookings's original character, but the coast is as gorgeous as ever, bookending the town with scenes of breathtaking beauty. To the northwest are the Samuel H. Boardman and Harris Beach State Parks; to the east are the verdant Siskiyou Mountains, deeply cut by the Chetco and Winchuck Rivers.

▶ **Wildlife Viewing.** To find nature's elusive creatures, charter a boat from the harbor to watch the gray whale migration in January or spy the pods from one of the vantage points along the highway. At dusk or dawn, head to Rowdy Creek or Winchuck River (southeast of Brookings, inland from Highway 101) to view deer and elk. In late February, squawking Aleutian Canada geese gather at Lake Earl at the mouth of the Smith River. Other area birds include tufted puffins, spotted owls, marbled murrelets, bald eagles, ospreys, and red-tailed hawks.

In front of the historical museum is the largest Monterey cypress in the United States.

 From the Pioneer Days. Chetco Valley Historical Museum (Museum Road, (503) 469-6651), the oldest standing structure in the area, is a former way station and trading post. Dating back to 1857, the wooden home contains much of what you'd expect – a spinning wheel and several old sewing machines, a trunk from 1706, photographs depicting the harbor area's rich history, Native American artifacts, a hoary moonshine still – and the exceptional: an iron casting of a face, which some believe to be the image of Queen Elizabeth I, perhaps left behind in the 1500s by Sir Francis Drake. Open from mid-March to November. Free.

 As a center for flower growing, Brookings celebrates an annual Azalea Festival on Memorial Day weekend. But for fresh flowers year-round, look for the sign to Flora Pacifica's viewing garden and flower mart (15447 Ocean View Drive; (800) 877-9741 or (503) 469-9741), south of town. Many of their creations incorporate wild greens responsibly harvested from the surrounding woodlands. Wreaths made from all-natural materials are also for sale. Hydrangeas, statice, artemesias, pennyroyal, salas, myrtle, as well as herbs grow in the farm's maintained gardens.

≥ Smoked from the Sea. The Great American Smokehouse and Seafood Company (15657 Highway 101; (503) 469-6903 or (800) 828-FISH) has Indian-style smoked salmon jerky strips, smoked tuna and jerky, jam, lox, and a variety of other seafood, smoked and fresh. No doubt about it, at $25 per pound the salmon jerky is pricey, but so good. Smoky, rich, and peppery, it's worth the couple of bucks for a Magic Marker–size stick to nosh on. The place prides itself on dolphin-free products, hook-and-line fishing, and absolute freshness. They ship anywhere.

≥ Redwoods. The Brookings-Harbor region contains the greatest diversity of conifers in the world, among them redwoods, Brewer spruce, myrtlewood, and plants associated with serpentine soils. Nearby hiking trails provide the best opportunity to see these riparian relics. The scenic Oregon Coast Trail connects Loeb State Park, 8 miles up the Chetco River on North Bank Road, with the Redwood Nature Trail for a 2-mile hike through myrtlewoods and redwoods.

The Bombsite Trail, 18 miles east of Brookings, is highly recommended by locals. Located on Forest Service Road #1205 after spur #260 (take South Bank Road to Mt. Emily Road), it is 1 mile long and meanders through an old-growth redwood forest. At the end is the site that was hit by two Japanese incendiary bombs during World War II. Fifty years later, the pilot, Nubuo Fujita, visited Brookings and donated his family's 400-year-old samurai sword to the city as a gesture of "trans-Pacific amity."

 Azalea State Park, north of downtown Brookings, is best known for its gorgeous blooms in May and for the Azalea Festival, held here on Memorial Day weekend. Recently the 36-acre park added a fantasyland playground, with turrets, slides, and wooden skyways that smaller kids will love. Take the short path up to the gazebo to fully survey the landscaped grounds, or sit at one of the handmade myrtlewood picnic tables to watch the butterflies (plentiful in early summer) flit from flower to flower.

 Just 1 mile north of Brookings, fearless and friendly gulls mind Harris Beach State Park, which has overnight camping (151 sites) and day-use facilities in addition to great wraparound views. A seascape painter's dream, the park's driftwood coastline is dotted with gnarled basalt outcroppings with such descriptive names as Hunchback and Whales Head.

Restaurants

HOG WILD CAFE

This boutiquey restaurant has gone a bit wild on the pig theme, what with pig dolls, pig cups, and a sign that reads, "Please don't hog the bath-

Several miles north of Brookings, the Natural Bridges Cove viewpoint along Highway 101 has a paved walkway at the south end of the lot that leads through fern, fir, old-growth spruce, and alder to a monumental overlook of crashing surf and rock archways. The cove is part of Samuel H. Boardman State Park, and the Oregon Coast Trail leads off from here, north and south.

room." You'll find jambalaya, veggie lasagne, and Cajun meat loaf on the regular menu, plus a good many blackboard items, such as a vegetable frittata or prime rib sandwich. The biggest pigs show up on Wednesdays for the barbecue dinner. *West side of Hwy 101, 1 mile south of Brookings-Harbor bridge; (503) 469-8869; 16158 Hwy 101 S, Harbor; $; beer and wine; AE, DIS, MC, V; local checks only; breakfast, lunch every day, dinner Wed-Sat.*

RUBIO'S ☆

The salsa is outstanding; you can buy jars of it here and elsewhere in Brookings. But the restaurant itself is the only place you can get Rubio's incredible chiles rellenos and chile verde. And – wow – the seafood à la Rubio combines fresh lingcod, scallops, and prawns in a butter, garlic, wine, and jalapeño sauce. Avoid the greasy entomatada. There's a drive-thru for take-out orders, when it's just too busy inside. *At the north end of town; (503) 469-4919; 1136 Chetco Ave, Brookings; $$; beer and wine; AE, DIS, MC, V; local checks only; lunch, dinner Tues-Sun (Tues-Sat in winter).*

Lodgings

CHETCO RIVER INN ⋆⋆

Expect a culture shock: the fishing retreat sits on 35 acres of a peninsula wrapped by the turquoise Chetco River, 17 miles east of Brookings (pavement ends after 14 miles) and 6 miles from a phone. There's a radio-phone operator, but forget private conversations. The lovely deep green marble floors are a purposefully practical choice for muddy fishermen's boots. The place is not so remote that you can't read by safety propane lights and watch TV via satellite (there's even a VCR). The large, open main floor offers views of the river, myrtle-wood groves, and wildlife. Innkeeper Sandra Brugger will provide early-riser breakfast service, pack a deluxe sack lunch, or serve an exemplary five-course dinner on request. All told, this is getting away from it all in fishing style. *Follow North Bank Rd 16 miles, left after South Fork Bridge, take second guest driveway on left; (503) 469-8128 (radiophone), (800) 327-2688 (Pelican Bay Travel); 21202 High Prairie Rd, Brookings, OR 97415; $$; MC, V; checks OK.*

Cheap Sleep. Much has changed since the Chetco Inn became the talk of the town three-quarters of a century ago, when luminaries such as Clark Gable and Carole Lombard made the new electric and steam-heated hotel their weekend retreat. Unfortunately, the matronly 44-room edifice is a shadow of its former self, but it has retained its character. And it's being renovated, albeit at a snail's pace. Downtown at 417 Fern St; (503) 469-5347; PO Box 1386, Brookings, OR 97415; $; AE, DIS, MC, V; no checks.

HOLMES SEA COVE BED AND BREAKFAST

Jack and Lorene Holmes offer two guest rooms on the lower level of their cozy ocean-view home north of town (as well as a private guest studio). The home sits on a waterfront bluff, with a trail that winds its way down to the ocean, and to a private park with picnic tables. Lorene brings a continental breakfast to your room. *Take Hwy 101 north to Dawson Rd, left to Holmes Dr; (503) 469-3025; 17350 Holmes Dr, Brookings, OR 97415; $$; MC, V; checks OK.*

BEACHFRONT INN

Sure, it's only a Best Western, but if you want an oceanfront motel room in Brookings, this is the closest you can get. Nothing special besides the view and the beach. Some units have kitchens; one has a two-person Jacuzzi. *On Lower Harbor Rd, south of the Port of Brookings; (503) 469-7779 or (800) 468-4081; PO Box 2729, Brookings, OR 97415; $$; AE, DC, DIS, MC, V; checks OK.*

Index

A, B

The Adobe Resort, 84, 85
Anchorage Motel, 51
Andrea's, 121
Arch Cape, 28
The Argonauta Inn, 33
Astoria, 3–17
Astoria Inn Bed and Breakfast, 15
Azalea State Park, 143
Bandon, 113–25
Bandon Boatworks, 122
Bandon Wayside Motel, 124
Battle Rock Motel, 131
Bay City, 41–42
The Bay House, 57
Beach Loop Road, 117
Beachfront Inn, 146
Beachwood Bed and Breakfast, 24
The Bistro, 30
Blackberry Inn, 108
Blue Hen Cafe, 94
Blue Heron Bistro, 106
Blue Sky Cafe, 39
The Boarding House, 23
Boice-Cope County Park, 117
Boiler Bay State Park, 64
Bombsite Trail, 143
The Brass Rail, 103
Brookings, 139–46
Brown Squirrel Hostel, 74
Bullards Beach State Park, 117, 118

Burd's Nest Inn Bed and Breakfast, 86

C

Cafe de la Mer, 29
Cafe Uniontown, 13
Camp Westwind, 60
Cannon Beach, 26–34
Cannon Beach Hotel, 33
Canyon Way Restaurant and Bookstore, 71
Cape Blanco State Park, 114
Cape Cod Cottages, 87
Cape Kiwanda, 43, 44, 47, 48
Cape Lookout, 43, 44
Cape Meares Lighthouse, 44
Cape Meares State Park, 43, 44
Cape Perpetua, 80, 82
Cape Perpetua Scenic Area, 81
Cape Sebastian State Park, 135
The Captain's Table, 135
Cascade Head, 51
Cassandra's, 39
Castaway by the Sea, 130
Cathedral Tree Trail, 8
CB's Bistro (Sixes River Hotel), 128
Chameleon Cafe, 58
Channel House, 65
Charleston, 108–13

The Chelan, 53
Chetco River Inn, 145
Chetco Valley Historical
    Museum, 141
Chez Jeannette, 60
Clementine's Bed and
    Breakfast, 16
Cliff House Bed and
    Breakfast, 78
Cloverdale, 47–50
Columbia River, 4, 6, 12
Columbia River Maritime
    Museum, 6
Columbian Cafe, 12
Coos Bay, 104–08
Coos Bay Manor Bed and
    Breakfast Inn, 107
Coquille Point Wildlife
    Park, 118
Crest Motel, 15

D, E, F

Darlingtonia Botanical
    Wayside, 93
Dean Creek Elk Viewing
    Area, 98
Depoe Bay, 63–66
Dooger's, 22
Dory Cove, 57
Drift Creek Wilderness, 78
Driftwood Beach, 75
Ecola State Park, 19, 28
Edgewater Cottages, 87
Edwin K Bed and Break-
    fast, 95
Floras Lake House Bed
    and Breakfast, 129
Florence, 89–96
Fogarty Creek State Park,
    64

Fort Clatsop National
    Memorial, 5
Fort Stevens State Park,
    10, 11
Franklin Street Station, 16

G, H, I

Garibaldi, 41–42
Gearhart, 17–19
Gleneden Beach, 60–62
Gold Beach, 131–39
Gold Beach Resort, 138
Grateful Bread Bakery, 49
Gull Haven Lodge, 96
Harp's, 122
Harris Beach State Park,
    143
Hatfield Marine Science
    Center, 69
Haystack Rock, 28
Hebo Lake, 48
Heceta Head, 81
Highlands Bed and Break-
    fast, 103
Hog Wild Cafe, 143
Holmes Sea Cove Bed and
    Breakfast, 146
Home by the Sea Bed and
    Breakfast, 130
House on the Hill, 46
Hudson House Bed and
    Breakfast, 50
Humbug Mountain State
    Park, 126
Inn at Face Rock, 123
The Inn at Manzanita, 40
Inn at Nesika Beach, 138
Inn at Otter Crest, 65

J, K, L

Jarboe's, 38
Jewell Meadows Wildlife
    Area, 10
Johnson House Bed and
    Breakfast, 95
Jot's Resort, 139
Kalmiopsis Wilderness,
    134
Klootchy Creek Park, 20
Kum-Yon's, 106
La Serre, 83
Lazy Susan Cafe, 31
Lewis and Clark Interpre-
    tive Center, 12
Lighthouse Bed and Break-
    fast, 123
Lincoln City, 54–60

M, N

Manzanita, 34–41
Maxwell Mountain, 44
Midtown Cafe, 31
Mount Hebo, 49
Natural Bridges Cove, 144
Neahkanie Mountain, 35
Nehalem Bay State Park,
    37
Neskowin, 51–54
Neskowin Scenic Route,
    52
New Morning Coffee-
    house, 84
Newport, 66–75
North Bend, 102–04
Nor'Wester, 136
Nye Beach, 66

O, P

Ocean House, 73
Oceanside, 42–47

Ona Beach State Park, 75
Oregon Coast Aquarium,
    70
Oregon Coast Trail, 11, 44,
    110, 127, 142, 144
Oregon Dunes National
    Recreation Area, 90,
    97
Oregon House, 88
Oregon Institute of Marine
    Biology, 112
Oregon Islands National
    Wildlife Refuge, 110
Oswald West State Park,
    35, 37
Otis, 51–53
Otis Cafe, 52
Pacific City, 47–51
Pacific Sands, 54
Pacific Way Bakery and
    Cafe, 18
Palmer House, 59
Port Orford, 125–31
Portside, 112
Prehistoric Gardens, 127
Proposal Rock, 52
Puget Island, 7

Q, R

Quatat Marine Park, 21
Redwood Nature Trail, 142
Reedsport, 97–99
Rio Cafe, 14
Riverhouse Restaurant, 49
Riverside Inn Bed and
    Breakfast, 25
Robert Straub State Park,
    48
Rogue River, 132, 133
Rogue River Trail, 134

Roseanna's Oceanside Cafe, 46
Rosebriar Hotel, 17
Rubio's, 144

S

Saddle Mountain State Park, 20
St. Perpetua Trail, 80
Salishan Lodge, 61
Salmon River Cafe, 58
Sandbeach Campground, 45
Sandlake, 45
Sea Lions Caves, 82
Sea Quest Bed and Breakfast, 84
Sea Sprite Motel, 34
Sea Star Bistro, 120
Seal Rock, 75–77
Seaside, 19–26
Seaside Inn and International Hostel, 25
The See Vue, 88
Shilo Inn (Seaside Oceanfront), 24
The Ship Inn, 13
Shore Acres State Park, 110
Siskiyou National Forest, 134
South Beach State Park, 70
South Slough National Estuarine Research Reserve, 111
Stephanie Inn, 32
Strawberry Hill, 81
Sunset Bay State Park, 109
Sunset Motel, 125
Sylvia Beach Hotel, 72

T, U, V

Three Capes Scenic Drive, 43, 44, 47
Tillamook, 42–46
Tillamook Head, 19, 28
Tillicum Beach Campground, 78
Tolovana Park, 26–34
Truculent Oyster Restaurant and Peg Leg Saloon, 129
Tu Tu'Tun Lodge, 137
Twilight Eagle Sanctuary, 10
Umpqua Discovery Center, 97
Umpqua Dunes Trail, 100
Umpqua Lighthouse State Park, 100
Upper Nestucca River Recreation Area, 45
The Vikings, 75
Vista Sea Cafe, 22

W, X, Y, Z

Waldport, 77–79
Wayside Lodge, 89
West Coast Game Park, 119
The Whale's Tale, 71
Winchester Bay, 99–102
Windermere Motel, 124
Yachats, 79–89
Yachats 804 Trail, 80
Yaquina Head Outstanding Natural Area, 68
Yuzen, 76
Ziggurat, 85